Abide

Abide

Keeping Vigil with the Word of God

Macrina Wiederkehr, OSB

LITURGICAL PRESS
Collegeville, Minnesota

www.litpress.org

10 11 12

Library of Congress Cataloging-in-Publication Data

Wiederkehr, Macrina.
    Abide : keeping vigil with the Word of God / Macrina Wiederkehr.
      p. cm.
    Includes bibliographical references.
    ISBN 978-0-8146-3383-0 — ISBN 978-0-8146-3958-0 (ebook)
    1. Bible—Meditations.   2. Catholic Church—Prayers and devotions.
  I. Title.

BS491.5.W52   2011
242'.5—dc23   2011028702

*Dedicated to
the Word of God,
abiding in you.*

Contents

Foreword

When I found your words, I devoured them;
they became my joy and the happiness of my heart. (Jer 15:16)

Jeremiah, the great prophet of Israel, was torn between his devotion to God and his utter terror at proclaiming the difficult message that God's people needed to hear. He begged the Lord for relief from his duties, and yet embraced his prophetic mission with a zeal that was singular. Why? Because God's words had become Jeremiah's nourishment; he knew no joy or happiness could match the power of God that filled him.

Jeremiah wrestled with the Word of God, a sometimes difficult but always life-giving Word. He is not the only one to do so. Our Bibles are filled with stories of those who sought God's voice and responded, sometimes haltingly and sometimes poignantly, to the sound of the divine. They listened for God's voice so often that it became familiar.

We do the same. When we allow God's words to wash over us, we cannot help but be transformed, however slowly, until finally we want to consume the sacred words. This book, appropriately titled *Abide*, invites us to sit with the Word of God, to remain there for a while so that it can begin to seep into us. It reminds us that receiving the Word of God is not a matter of intellect but of presence, our lingering presence in the company of God, and God's desire to be present with and for us.

In 1991, Macrina Wiederkehr, OSB, began writing a regular column for the *Stepping Stones* newsletter of Little Rock Scripture Study. From the beginning, she set out to invite readers into a relationship with God through the words of Scripture. Her columns are titled "Romancing the Word" and in each one she reminds us that when we pray with Scripture, we place ourselves knowingly in relationship with God. These original columns form the background for this book that you hold in your hands.

In the reflections that Sr. Macrina offers, you will notice the rich Benedictine heritage of *lectio divina* as well as evidence of artful attention to lived experience. This is the kind of book that can be picked up for a short while, allowing just a few pages at a time to penetrate your being. This book will invite you to stillness and wonder, and sometimes to wrestling and embracing.

Cackie Upchurch
Director, Little Rock Scripture Study

Acknowledgments

The Gift you have received, give as a gift. (see Matt 10:8)

This book is a gift and I am indebted to many gift-givers who have assisted me in the shaping of these pages as well as teaching me to abide.

I am grateful for the gift of

- the Little Rock Scripture Study staff and their tireless efforts to offer the Word of God to seekers throughout the world: Judy Hoelzeman, who in 1991 invited me to write a column for the *Stepping Stones* newsletter; Cackie Upchurch, director, and Susan McCarthy, newsletter editor, who have been encouraging mentors in this project;

- Mary Ann Soerries, Joyce Rupp, Elise Forst, Beth Fritsch, and Diana Squibb for their wise suggestions about rearranging words;

- my Benedictine community, Fr. David McKillin, Barbara Bock, Rachel Dietz, Kay Pope, and Karen Ewan for the little ways (often unknown to them) they teach me to abide;

- Liturgical Press, with special mention of Hans Christoffersen, Lauren L. Murphy, and my editor Stephanie Lancour, as well as all those behind the scenes;

- and finally for my newly discovered editor Mary Ann Soerries, who, although not a professional, became my primary editor for this work. As she faithfully perused these chapters making valuable suggestions for improvement, I kept saying to her, "People get paid for what you are doing." Nevertheless, she did it as gift.

The Gift you have received, give as a gift.

Introduction

Long before I knew anything about the Word of God, I found words intriguing. As a child I took delight in rearranging words into phrases and patterns, stories and poems. Perhaps, even then, I was romancing the Word. I was discovering that words bless. They move and dance and sing. They abide. They absorb and unite. They inspire. Words invite us to feel included, loved, honored. They call us to play and to work. They teach, comfort, praise. They forgive. They ask us to be authentic and true. They summon us to go deeper into the mystery of our lives. They teach us compassion and love. They make us laugh and cry. They draw us into the romance of life. Words can also destroy, wound, and kill the spirit. They can reject and ridicule. They can torment and make us believe that we are less than we are. Words are powerful; we can use them for good or for evil. Our words have power to bless or distress others. When we speak a word, it cannot be unspoken.

When our words are united to the Word of God, the result is a new creation. We are born into creativity, for ultimately we have come from the womb of God, the Source of life. The Word that spoke us into life was the Word of God. There is power in every word God speaks and since each one of us is a word of God, there is power in our words also. This is why it is so important for us to attend the Word. Pay attention to the words you speak. Pay attention to the words spoken by God. Only with attention

1

will we discover the power in the Word that enables us to call it the Word of God.

Keeping Vigil with the Word

In the Gospel of John Jesus directs us, "Remain in me, as I remain in you" (15:4). Here is an invitation to make the Word of God your home. This book of scriptural reflections encourages you to keep vigil with the Word each day so that you become more aware of the Holy Mystery keeping vigil with you. Thus as you open the pages of your heart to the transforming power of God's Word, a depth within you makes itself known and cries out for continued nurturing.

I love the story told in the first chapter of the Gospel of John (vv. 35-42). We see John the Baptist pointing his disciples in the direction of Jesus. The two disciples of John then begin following along behind Jesus. When Jesus sees them following and asks them, "What are you looking for?" they inquire, "where are you staying?" (v. 38). Jesus' answer, "Come, and you will see" (v. 39), can be an invitation to each of us to move deeper into our romance with the Word of God. The quest for a deeper relationship with the Holy Mystery we call God requires more than just asking questions about the dwelling place of God. We must be willing to be a home for the Word of God. Likewise, the Word becomes our abiding place, our abode. It is the space in our lives where we practice being rather than doing; it is the space where we remain in Jesus as he remains in us. There is no way to arrive at this place except through the gentle practice of romancing the Word of God.

In light of the story of the first disciples being called, I offer you two questions as guides for your transformational journey:

- *What are you looking for?* This is the question Jesus asked the two disciples who were tagging along behind him. Tagging along wasn't enough! A little more commitment was needed. However, at this point the disciples didn't have a clue about Jesus' identity. They were merely following him because John the Baptist pointed him out and said, "Behold, the Lamb of God." Curiosity is a good beginning; at least, they were looking in his direction. Nevertheless, in order to truly become a disciple of Jesus, our following must eventually become a choice of our own. In this question Jesus is trying to find out what it is they are seeking. He is curious about their hearts' deepest desire. Their counter question to Jesus is personal and probing.

- *Where are you staying?* Where is your dwelling place? Where is your home? It may be a rude awakening for the two disciples to discover that Jesus cannot tell them where he is staying by means of describing a physical environment. Perhaps Jesus is hoping they will eventually discover that he lives in communion with the one he calls Abba. His true dwelling is not in a physical place. He abides in the Holy Mystery. As they slowly become his disciples this is where they must learn to stay—not in a place but in the heart of a Mystery too deep for words.

These two questions are good spiritual guides for our quest to the home of the Beloved. We find the way on the way.

As you pray the Scriptures each day, listen to Jesus asking you, "What are you looking for?" And just what are you looking for as you spend time with the Word of God? If I were to respond to that question, I would probably answer something like this: "I'm looking for a relationship with God, a communion with Christ that shows itself in the way I live." Although that is my answer today, next week it might be a little different. Our answer will come out of our lived experience as well as what is being revealed to us each time we come to the table of the Word of God.

Lectio Divina: **How to Keep Vigil**

These reflections have been gathered from my morning hours of keeping vigil with the Word of God. In the Benedictine tradition we call this form of monastic prayer *lectio divina*. In the monastic way of abiding with the Word we do not read the Scripture text to obtain information. The careful reading of the text is for the purpose of opening our hearts to be formed by the Word of God. We listen to the words so carefully that even our reading becomes a prayer. Sometimes we memorize short passages from the text so that we may more easily carry them with us throughout the day.

Here are a few suggestions for you as you entrust yourself to this way of prayer. As you begin your encounter with these meditations on the Word of God, spend some personal time with each text before reading my reflection on that text. Find the Scripture passage assigned to you in your Bible. Open the Scriptures to that particular text and then, WAIT.

Waiting may seem like an unnecessary constraint, yet the Scriptures are filled with assertions about the goodness of waiting. "For you I wait all the long day, because of your goodness, LORD" (Ps 25:5). You are invited to wait before the Word. You are not in a hurry. Are you waiting for the Holy Spirit? Yes and no! The Spirit is already present, so why are you waiting? Perhaps you are waiting for yourself to show up. Your body may be present but what about the roving mind?

A few moments of waiting can help you remember that this is a consecrated time, blessed and set apart. Your waiting may enable you to sense the presence of the Holy Spirit. Most of us do not like to wait; we are tempted to plunge right into our work, even into our spiritual work. Yet, there is so much grace in waiting. You are keeping vigil with your longing to be transformed by the Word of God. Discover the grace of waiting. Learn to wait! When you sense a readiness in your soul, READ.

Read the Scripture text slowly, committing yourself to see it through to the end even if you decide midway through the reading that it does not speak to you. Perhaps you have prayed with this text many times before; you want something new and more exciting. Stand in faith and read it anyway. Your only assignment is to be faithful to this pathway of words. When you have finished reading the assigned Scripture text, then it is time for you to LISTEN OBEDIENTLY.

Does obedience to the Word of God seem to be an outdated assignment? You were probably expecting the task of meditating on the assigned Scripture. In a sense this is exactly what I am asking you to do; I'm just using different language. Many of us are not eager for obedience. The invitation to obedience often evokes memories of unhealthy forms of submission. The obedience referred to here, though, is a listening so deep we are drawn into the Spirit of Jesus and given a wisdom that enables us to know how to respond to the Word. It is an obedience that is revelatory.

As I grow in the way of *lectio divina* I find it an enriching practice to ask the Holy Spirit to show me how to be obedient to the Word of God. Saint Benedict asks us to listen with the ear of our hearts. You are being invited to be formed by the Word of God. Read the text a second time, opening your heart to the deeper ways you are being called to obedience. If it is helpful, journal about the particular ways this Scripture is inviting you into a greater spiritual maturity. Let the words paint icons in your mind. Envision yourself being drawn into a deeper union with God. How can the message of this Scripture text teach you to abide? Having reflected on obedient listening to God's Word, it is now time to PRAY.

Do you know how to pray? Only the Holy Spirit can teach you to pray. I am not giving you instructions on how to pray. In whatever way the energy of the Spirit moves you, lean in that direction. Look once again at the ways God has spoken to you in this Scripture text; hold it dear and pray. With or without words, pray. Your prayer may lead you quite naturally into the final movement of *lectio*, which is simply to ABIDE.

This is a beautiful moment spent in pure contemplative presence with the Beloved. This is love. "Remain in me, as I remain in you" (John 15:4). "Be still and know that I am God" (Ps 46:10, NRSV). Dwell. Remain in love. ABIDE.

These are only a few suggestions of ways for you to commit yourself to the Word of God: *Wait* in silence before the Word. *Read* contemplatively. Be faithful to the reading whether you are moved by it or not. *Listen obediently* to the text. Discern how the Word is calling you to a greater obedience. *Pray* as the Holy Spirit leads you. And finally, *ABIDE.* You are being invited to enter into an abiding presence with the Word of God.

The Sacramentality of Our Daily Quest for God

In these reflections on the Word of God we will be praying with the sacramentality of our lives and our faithful efforts in renewing our spiritual selves as we continue our quest for God.

Chapter 1 offers us opportunities to reflect on the magnetic attraction we experience as we are constantly drawn toward the divine. In chapter 2 we are invited to be faithful to our innate yearning for God as we search for ways to move more deeply into relationship with God. Chapter 3 encourages us to find beauty and sacramental grace right in the midst of our ordinary daily struggles. The fourth chapter attempts to support us in the difficult task of living truly committed lives. Finally, the fifth chapter invites us into the conversion experience of returning to our original love. Each chapter ends with a poetic reflection, which can serve as a summary of the chapter and as a way to review the core themes with which we have prayed.

These reflections were written while I was enjoying ordinary places—lakes, mountains, meadows, gardens, churches, coffee shops, dining rooms, retreat centers, and hospitals. Most, though, were written while I was in my daily place of prayer—beside my window overlooking my beloved sycamore tree, which has stood through all kinds of weather.

As my faith life matures, I sense a deepening reverence for the Word of God. A scene from Pete Hamill's novel *Snow in August* describes the reverence I am beginning to feel. A boy is teaching English to Rabbi Hirsch. Michael, the young teacher, observes that when he corrects the pronunciation of the rabbi, the old mistake is never made again. The rabbi treats each word with astounding reverence.

> The rhythms of the sentences were often wrong; the verbs were in the wrong place. But the rabbi treated words as if they were jewels. He caressed them, handled them with his tongue, repeated them with delight, turned them over for a view from another angle.[1]

The rabbi's reverence in reading the words of Scripture throws light on a very dear moment. I am able to observe the rabbi with his sacred text just as I might gaze upon a rare painting. I too would like to treat each word as a jewel, treasuring it and beholding it from many different views. I want to turn the words over in my heart as a plough turns over the soil to welcome the seed. I would like to breathe upon and into the words much like the poet Mary Oliver breathes into her poems. That is the kind of presence I desire.

If this poetic language of turning words over like jewels and breathing into them is too dramatic for you, please understand that I am only trying to underline the importance of radical presence. Drawing near to the Word of God requires a very special kind of presence.

Before you begin your journey through these reflections on the Word of God, I offer you yet one more way to approach the assigned Scripture texts. On some days, stand as a pilgrim before the Word of God. Visualize your movement down the path of words as a pilgrimage. The places where you choose to stop for further reflection are your pilgrim sites, your holy places along the way. This is an insightful and creative way to keep vigil with the Word.

It is not easy to find the Word of God in the midst of a jumble of words. The secret is connection. A community of words connects with each other and somehow in that connection we discern God's Word for us. Praying with the white space between the words, sentences, and paragraphs is also important. The artist in us needs white space—our place of waiting, listening, and being. White space is the womb and the tomb in which we abide. We will experience birth, life, and death there, as we keep vigil with the Word of God.

Be open to God's Word blossoming everywhere. Walk with awareness through the forests, parks, and gardens, along the seashore, or down a busy city street. The Word of God is near you. Climb a mountain and the Word will meet you. Move mindfully through your daily work tasks—the Word is at your fingertips. Celebrate the Eucharist with a community of struggling believers. You will be enfolded in God's creative Word.

Every person you encounter during the hours of your day is a word that God has spoken into the world. You too are one of God's spoken words. And now God speaks through you.

Chapter One

Drawn Like a Magnet to the Divine

The German poet Rainer Maria Rilke speaks of our quest for God as a homesickness we cannot escape.[1] These words ring true in my personal exploration into the mystery of the divine. My efforts to abide in the Word are sometimes accompanied by a little loneliness. The Word of God is like a poultice for the homesick heart. Scripture has the potential to be an agent of healing if I practice abiding in the sacred words, as opposed to simply reading them.

When I am able to approach the Word of God expecting some kind of conversion, I experience a little death. The Hebrew people believed that one could not see the face of God and live. In light of that belief perhaps the dying I experience should delight me. When I am confronted by God's Word, I am sometimes able to recognize that some change is needed in my life. Ordinarily I name this piece of growth, transformation. Of course, the other side of transformation is that until I am able to integrate the change into my life, with a certain acceptance, it feels more like death.

I am a seeker on the Christ path. I am intimately acquainted with the transformative power of words. Like a mystery story the words of Scripture keep alluring me and challenging me. When I turn to Scripture for prayer, I am nourished with words—mysterious, captivating, enlightening, and saving words. Fundamentalist

Christians often ask me if I have been saved. Although I know what they mean, I tend to look at salvation as a process, rather than a "once upon a time" event. Every time I sit down with the Word of God, with the kind of presence Jesus modeled, something turns over in the ground of my being that feels like a little salvation. I experience the process of "being saved" from my own triviality. I am saved by the Word of God.

The Scripture reflections in this beginning chapter of *Abide* focus on our attraction to the divine. A magnetic force keeps drawing us toward the eternal. Not everyone experiences this attraction in the same way. The poetic ones among us often use language that is not helpful to those persons who are more pragmatic. On some days we struggle to feel anything—certainly not some magnetic mystery tugging us toward intimacy. The most important question is, are we accessible? Can God get in? Or, is our need for certainty so overpowering that it becomes a prison walling out even the divine? Whatever our inclination, God is always calling us beyond what we can see with the naked eye.

You are invited to begin these reflections by praying with Scripture texts that suggest an authentic receptivity to God. These "words" have the potential of drawing you like a magnet to the divine. You will need to surrender your craving for certainty. As you gaze into the face of God you will not always know whether to call it life or death.

1. Desire for God

Prayerfully read Psalm 63.

> *O God, you are my God—for you I long!*
> *For you my body yearns; for you my soul thirsts,*
> *Like a land parched, lifeless, and without water. (v. 2)*

Read these words again. Listen to the tone of longing in the voice of the psalmist. If you have ever experienced the miracle that takes place when you water a plant that has begun to wither from lack of moisture, you will understand why earth's longing for water is compared to soul's longing for God.

Young trees and plants dry up from lack of rain. So too our spirits wither when we deprive ourselves of the healthy spiritual practice of abiding with the Word of God. Time set aside for *lectio divina* is like water for the soul.

Sometimes when I sit down to pray, I sense a deep stirring within, as though something very old yet not fully understood resides in me. This mysterious something that makes its presence known is so vague and yet so numinous. My desire to tap the eternal becomes all-encompassing in my moments of silent prayer with the Word of God.

Could this stirring within actually be God who lives and moves and loves in me? Does the part of me that often limps along halfheartedly need to learn to connect with that part of me which is most like God? Do I need to offer hospitality to everything within me that yearns for completion? How can I be faithful to my desire for God?

This I know to be true: an infinite yearning encircles me like the well-worn comforter I snuggle up with on cold winter nights.

It is during my times of silence that I am most powerfully moved by a deep yearning for God. This very longing is a gift from heaven. Like a magnet, we are constantly drawn to the divine. We ache for the eternal. This age-old longing is surely what the author of Psalm 63 was experiencing. Desire for God permeates this psalm. Each of us houses an ancient longing. Our longing, however, has a tendency to grow weary. During these weary times, it needs a blessing. When our river of desire for God grows shallow, it needs to be deepened. When our flame of love grows dim, it needs to be rekindled. This deepening and rekindling of our lives is necessary in order for us to be the blessing we were created to be.

> *I will bless you as long as I live;*
> *I will lift up my hands, calling on your name. (v. 5)*

How can we call upon God's name when we are weary? How can we get our longing renewed so that we may faithfully follow it home to God? A personal experience speaks to me about the importance of allowing the faithfulness of others to bless us.

Early morning in my monastery is sacred for me. The silence before Lauds and Eucharist is a welcoming space for my soul. This is one of my cherished times of the day. I often spend part of this time in the monastic dining room enjoying a cup of coffee as morning rays stream through the windows. One morning during this special silence, that ancient longing stirred within.

It happened like this. Sitting quietly in the subdued morning light, I became aware of another sister on the far side of the dining room having her own quiet time. A contemplative beauty surrounded her as she sat with her Bible open, savoring the Word of God. The image of her praying was surprisingly moving. I came to the dining room early each morning that week. Morning after morning she was prayerfully present to me. Apparently this was her coffee and *lectio* moment. One morning I unexpectedly found myself moved to tears. Again I became aware of an elusive ache arising in me. Later when I prayed about my tears trying to discern what was going on, I recalled something the storyteller Michael Mead once shared in an interview with *EarthLight* magazine.

Mead spoke about the importance of a younger person being mentored by an elder. Mentoring takes place, he suggests, when a young person sees in an older person a bright flame of life, which is a reminder of his or her own small flame. When these two flames connect, the younger person gets his or her flame blessed, while the older person moves into deeper wisdom. Michael Mead's words helped me to realize what was happening during my morning meditation in the cafeteria. My sister's faithfulness to her flame of life was blessing my own tired flame. My desire to be more faithful was being strengthened by her everyday faithfulness.

This experience exemplifies how God's blessing often comes in unexpected ways, and why it is so important for us to be "present" to the moment. The potential of a deeper relationship with the Holy Mystery we call God is always available. We may not be able to meditate through the watches of the night, yet there are many ways of being faithful to the heart's longing.

Pray for the kind of thirst that impels you to romance the Word of God. Make your home in the shadow of God's wings. Learn to wait for God with a deep trust. If you cling fast to the Word, you will store up enough energy to bless the fainthearted. Although desire for God is innate in every heart, this desire is not always evident. However, through prayer and practice, you can become a vessel of encouragement, stirring up new life in the hearts of those whose desire for God has weakened. You can move forward watering weary spirits and blessing tired flames.

> *O God, you are my God—for you I long!*
> *For you my body yearns; for you my soul thirsts,*
> *Like a land parched, lifeless, and without water. (v. 2)*

Reflection and Prayer

- Can you identify with the *yearning* referred to in this meditation? How would you describe your own desire for God? Try to give expression to your heart's longing by means of poetry, creative writing, or some work of art.

- What is your most recent experience of having your dried up spirit watered, your tired flame blessed? Who or what was the source of the blessing?

- Can you think of anyone in your life whose wavering flame needs a blessing? Do you have a blessing to spare?

Creative and Ever Faithful God,

Long have I lived in the shadow of your wings! In the stream of your living waters I have been refreshed. I have drunk deeply from the pages of Scripture. I have tried to make my home in you. In spite of your faithful presence and the many ways you have leaned toward me with love, I have not always been content. My yearning for you has led me in many directions and on strange pathways. Yet you always call me home, blessing my little flame of love, providing streams of healing water for my thirst, offering me new tributaries. Today I will drink from the stream of gratitude as I remember the ways you have guided me. Thank you for breathing me into each new day. Thank you for the many ways you rekindle my weary flame. I am grateful for that age-old yearning that keeps stirring in my heart. **Amen.**

2. Come to the Water

Prayerfully read Isaiah 55.

> *All you who are thirsty,*
> *come to the water!*
> *You who have no money . . .*
> *Come, without paying . . . (v. 1)*

Listen to the tenderness of these words. As you begin romancing the Word of God, you will notice that our romance begins with an invitation, which is often the way a romance begins. We are invited to come to the source and replenish our thirst and hunger. We are to come as we are. It doesn't matter if our pockets are empty. We cannot buy the Word of God. We are to receive it as gift. The only price we have to pay is to *show up* at the table of the Word, acknowledging our thirst for living water. The price we pay is our desire for communion with God.

When we sit at our dinner table, we expect to receive nourishment for our bodies. Our souls can also be fed at this table. In sharing both food and conversation, we are replenishing body and soul. By attentive presence to one another, we are offering the other hospitality. Is it possible to offer hospitality to someone and remain unchanged?

Is it possible to extend hospitality to the Word of God and remain unchanged? We offer hospitality to the Word by keeping company with it in our prayer and inviting it to companion us through the hours of the day. We offer hospitality to the Word when we lean toward it with the ear of our hearts, listening expectantly to its wisdom. Our abiding presence to the Word of God can bring about a profound transformation in our daily lives.

An enriching question from Dom Helder Camara deepens my desire for this daily transformation: *"Lord,"* he asks, *"what is the point of your presence if our lives do not alter?"*[2] As we are invited to the saving waters of God's Word in this fifty-fifth chapter of Isaiah, another provocative question is offered for our consideration: *"Why spend your money for what is not bread; your wages for what fails to satisfy?"* (v. 2). As simple as this question may seem to be, it is not an easy question to answer. Paul ponders a similar dilemma in his letter to the Romans when he cries out, *"What I do, I do not understand. For I do not do what I want, but I do what I hate"* (7:15). Paul too is questioning why he cannot be faithful to his deepest desires.

These very rich questions can serve as wonderful resource material for your prayer. Although you are being asked to pray these questions, you are not necessarily expected to answer them. Praying the question is an important part of *lectio divina.* Take it within your being for consideration. Look at it from many perspectives. Wait with it and, perhaps, walk with it. Prayerful questioning is a way of leading you into deeper reflection. Why do we *come to the water* if not to have our thirst quenched? What is the point of seeking God if we don't want to be found by God? Why spend so much of our precious time in places that do not nourish us? Why anguish over our desire for the divine if we are not willing to leap into the ocean of God?

If we come to the waters of God's Word with a willing spirit asking to be nourished, surely we can expect some kind of transformation. The change may be ever so small. It may be a *new insight* into why we give so much of our time to things that do not nourish us. It may be a passionate desire to deepen our relationship with God by spending more time ministering to the poor. The more we offer hospitality to the Word of God and welcome it into our heart space, the deeper our romance with God will be. We will experience healthy changes taking place in our daily lives.

Listen, that you may have life. (v. 3)

In both human and divine relationships, there can be no romance without a reverent listening to the other. When we make room in our lives for silence, the heaven and earth within us find each other. Then the Word of God is able to put down deep roots. These listening roots sense our desire for bonding with the Holy One. They know that the reason we accepted God's invitation to come into the arms of grace is because of our desire for a renewed life. They invite us into an even deeper abiding.

God's promise of renewing his covenant with Israel must be widened to include us. We too are intimately bonded with the Source of life. The relationship that was formed and celebrated at our baptism continues to flourish on our earthly pilgrimage. The invitation to seek God is renewed each day. We are reminded that just as the rain and snow listen to the roots that are waiting for water, so too God's Word hears our prayers and soaks into our waiting hearts, bringing us new life. All of this happens right here in the guesthouse of our hearts, where we keep vigil with the Word. We scramble through so many words looking for life until finally life comes in the one Word that finds us open, listening and waiting. Never underestimate the power of simply waiting for grace.

While praying this text from Isaiah, I began to understand that the Word of God is almost always trinitarian in its kinship to me. When I am able to leave behind my own fitful, limited thoughts and actually enter into the Word, I meet the trinitarian God. When I open myself to the Word of God, expecting to be transformed, something in me is *created anew*, *restored*, and *made holy*. I am embraced by *the Creator*, *the Redeemer*, and *the Sanctifier*. Through this embrace I am given the wisdom to allow the reshaping of my life. In this embrace I experience the intimacy of being drawn like a magnet into the Divine Presence.

Reflection and Prayer

- Is it possible to offer hospitality to another person and remain unchanged?

- Can you recall one moment from the past week when you opened your heart to another person? What did this gesture of kindness teach you about yourself and the other person?

- Is it possible to offer hospitality to the Word of God and remain unchanged? Can you remember a time in the past month when your presence to the Word of God taught you something about yourself? In what small way were you changed?

O Living Water of God's Word,

I come to the table of your Word hungry and thirsty, empty and hopeful, restless and wondering. If I embrace your daily Word, will you transform me? What will be the price of this transformation? Even as I ask this question I do not demand an answer. I am willing to risk living without answers. I ask only for the grace to rest in your presence like a seed in the darkness of the earth, like a child in its mother's womb. I offer the hospitality of a soul, ready to grow. Return this hospitality to me. Water the seed of my life with your amazing grace. **Amen.**

3. All I Want Is to Know Christ

Prayerfully read Philippians 3:7-16.

> *I have indeed been taken possession of by Christ. (v. 12)*

I walked at dawn—my favorite time to *romance the Word*. Shadows of night lingered briefly. Shades of day emerged slowly and quietly. How dear are these in-between times! During this morning's walk, it occurred to me that the seasons of the year were also speaking to me of the in-between times of winter and spring. At the threshold of this dawning day both seasons spoke to me. The slight nip of a winter wind invigorated me, encouraging me to pull up the hood of my jacket. The sight of budding trees showing faintly through the glow of dawn caused me to stand and gaze. These in-between times need to be savored.

During my walk, a prayer line from Philippians blessed and challenged me: *"I have indeed been taken possession of by Christ"* (v. 12). For many days now this text has been my breakfast. Before dawn, I read it aloud, slowly. I read it again in silence and then, I walk with it. In between day and night, in between winter and spring, I practice moving slowly, romancing the Word that becomes my morning prayer. The challenging truth of this message pours forth from my lips in many versions: "I have been grasped by Christ." "I have put away everything so that Christ may be my wealth." The pages of Scripture are filled with little prayers such as those mentioned above. The shortness of such phrases makes them wonderful prayers for meditative walks.

No matter what season you are in when you read this reflection, remember this truth: those *in-between times* are always with us. The paschal mystery, the dying and rising of Jesus, is the core of our lives as Christians. We live our lives in between the dying and rising. We have not fully experienced the dying. Nor have we lived the fullness of the risen life. We linger somewhere in between.

You and I, like Paul, have experienced moments of rising—of being grasped by Christ. We have known moments of crying out in the silence of our hearts, "all I want is to know Christ!" We have desired to live our lives in such a way that Christ will be our greatest wealth. We have prayed for the grace to die to our false selves and rise anew to life in Christ. Even if you don't recall actually praying for this grace, I would be very surprised if you haven't, at some time in your life, experienced a longing for Christ to be the center of your life. The longing is with you. It encircles you even when you are unaware of it.

Then suddenly you find yourself back in those in-between times. Distressing and boring as these in-between times of the season may seem, they can also be nourishing spaces for the soul. This waiting between dying and rising is like being in the tomb. It is a waiting room that is essential for spiritual growth. In this quiet tomb-place we feel, once again, that ancient tugging at the heart. We experience being drawn, like a magnet, to the divine.

As you linger in this waiting room, ask God to reveal your deepest desires to you. And while you wait in those in-between times, let this quote from *The Cloud of Unknowing* comfort you:

> *It is not what you are or what you have been that God sees with all merciful eyes, but what you desire to be.*[3]

These thoughts from Paul's letter to the Philippians about putting aside everything as useless so that Christ may be my greatest treasure, my prize, my wealth are quite radical. Even so,

I believe they might serve as a midlife passage for some of us. In midlife, we are drawn irresistibly toward the things that really matter. Our longing for things that rust and fade come less frequently. We have tasted enough of those *knowing Christ* moments to realize that they are beginning to have an enduring effect on us. This is something we notice as we grow older. The same thing happened to St. Paul. His experience of coming to know Christ led him to reassess everything in light of that knowledge. The things he once treasured seemed useless. He literally felt Christ taking possession of him.

No matter what season of life you are in, it will serve you well if you take some time to ponder the things that endure. Name the things in your life that truly matter. Reassess your life in light of eternity. Take a walk at dawn and open your eyes. The eternal may be closer than you have dared to believe. You do not have to surrender the beauty of the earth to know God. You need only to look at the things of this earth with the eyes of the Beloved. Christ is the garment you are called to put on each day. Christ is the union of death and life, the treasure whose name is Everlasting.

Reflection and Prayer

- Can you recall a time when you felt possessed by Christ? Savor that moment.

- As we grow older we often experience being able to surrender something that we once thought we couldn't live without. Have you experienced this?

- How might you robe yourself with Christ each day?

O Glance of God,

You, O Christ, are my wealth. All those things I thought I couldn't live without "dissolve" in a glance from you. They are nothing when considered in the larger light of your intimate presence. How difficult it has been to come to this moment! The moment of letting go! I, who have learned so well to hoard, grasp, clutch, and control! Now I want only to be grasped by you. All my possessions are empty when they become obstacles to my union with you. O Glance of God, prepare my heart for the Great Surrender. Enable me to surrender my ego self so that I may put on Christ. Then I will begin enjoying heaven on earth. **Amen.**

4. Recognizing the Beloved

Prayerfully read John 21:1-14.

"It is the Lord." (v. 7)

John, the disciple of Jesus often known as the Beloved Disciple, had a special relationship with Jesus. Because he is someone who obviously was drawn to the Lord, I will let him tell this story about a moment in his life when his love caused him to recognize Jesus. As you read my interpretation of John's words, no doubt you will remember times when the love in your own heart became a loving recognition.

John speaks:

Throughout the long night we toiled, catching nothing. We fisher folk know that nighttime is a good time for fishing. However, if the truth be known, the night we were experiencing was more than just the night that comes after the sun goes down. This darkness was deeper. It was a heaviness of the spirit. We knew we had to go on with our lives again just as you too have to go on living when someone you love dies. We were trying to discover how to find the hearts we had lost. We had "grown accustomed to his face." He had been our constant traveling companion. We had grown accustomed to his companionship, his stories, his eyes, the way he challenged us and his belief in us. We had grown accustomed to his constant, faithful love being there for us. Everything was different now! Even though he appeared to us, he never stayed around very long. We felt lost, confused, doubtful, fearful, and bewildered. We were wandering with no clear direction in view. Then suddenly, the darkness lifted.

Day was breaking. We could see more clearly. Someone was standing on the shore. We still didn't recognize him but he recognized us. The question he asked us might have added to our sense of failure had it not been for the loving concern in the tone of his voice—and that word, "children." "Children, have you caught anything to eat?" Children! We didn't look like children on the outside. Yet every person on our fishing boat was a frightened child. Somehow, our defenses down for a moment, we didn't mind being called children. The question, "have you caught anything to eat?" reminded us of hungers we had been unable to talk about with each other. "No," we answered, "we've worked through the night but we've caught nothing." "Cast your net off to the other side," he suggested.

How often someone standing at a distance, gazing on from another angle, can tell us where to look. Perhaps we had been too close to our sorrow, too close to the fears of the night to find success in our darkness. I only know that when we cast to the right side of the boat, we made a great catch. Then suddenly the sight of all those fish and the sound of his voice made a connection in my heart. At last I recognized the One who had recognized me all the while.

"It is the Lord," I cried out. Then Peter, beside himself with joy, jumped into the water. People in love do not always react in the same way. Peter leapt boldly and bodily into the water. I leapt lovingly and silently into the waters of my heart. Our fear was changed to love and, like children, we gathered around the charcoal fire to have breakfast with Jesus.

Having heard John's story, I invite you to gather, with Jesus, around the charcoal fire in your heart.

Reflection and Prayer

Prayerfully spend time with these questions as you continue to abide in the Word of God.

- Can you recall a time when you seemingly toiled all through the night and caught nothing? Claim that moment as a prayer and, even now, let Jesus change that darkness into dawn.

- Listen to Jesus asking you, "have you caught anything to eat?" List your recent sources of nourishment.

- Are you able to remember some dawn-breaking "it is the Lord" moments in your life? Name the people or circumstances that helped you to recognize God breaking through in your life and spend a few moments in gratitude.

- What present darkness in your life most needs to be blessed with the light of resurrection? Envision the light of dawn breaking into that darkness.

O Risen Christ,

When I search for you in the darkness
  Show me the light of your face.

When my darkness is too heavy
  Send me the dawn.

When I am dejected because of your absence
  Remind me to share my presence with someone.

When I am hungry for nourishment
  Invite me to breakfast.

When I cast my nets on the wrong side of life
  Come to my assistance.

When I do not recognize you
  Call me by name.

5. Pouring Out Your Heart of Love

Prayerfully read Luke 7:36-50.

You are a vessel of love and compassion.
Are you ready for the goodness of your life to be poured out?

A tall slender vessel sits on the shelf at my place of prayer. It isn't translucent enough to be an alabaster jar, yet as I pray with this particular Scripture, the jar enables me to focus on the life of Luke's nameless woman, the life of Jesus, and my own life. The alabaster jar is symbolic of a life that holds something precious about to be poured out. Pause for a moment to reflect on the vessel of your own life. Try to sense the goodness of your life that you sometimes dismiss or belittle. Remember too your tremendous potential to love, which, at times, you might question or even deny.

As you begin your prayer, focus on the penitent woman. See her entering the house of Simon. She is as transparent as the alabaster jar she carries. Simon's disapproval does not daunt her or detain her mission. She may well be a sinner but she is a sinner in love. She has heard Jesus' teaching. She has become a disciple.

I wonder: where did she first meet Jesus? Which words of his were the words that changed her life? What was the gospel that broke open the alabaster jar of her heart? When did she become a disciple?

We do not know when she first became a disciple, but this moment is certainly one of devoted discipleship. Attentive to her heart, she comes boldly into Simon's house. Her action is a kind of liturgical dance, but not everyone approves of her loving gesture. It is a moment of love gone beautifully wild—an adoring gesture, falling tears, flowing hair, the sealed jar breaking, the pouring out of costly ointment, the anointing of feet.

Jesus knows that the alabaster jar of her heart was broken long before she broke the alabaster jar of ointment. He is obviously touched by her dance of love. He is being anointed as much by the precious ointment of her faith as by the contents of the jar. Is he perhaps looking at this anointing as a preparation for his burial? Is he thinking, in any way, about the alabaster jar of his own life that he has been pouring out during his three years of ministry?

Jesus is anointed by a nameless woman's dance of love.

If we look through the gospels, we can clearly see that the life of Jesus has been a dance of love, a pouring out of life for others. Surely he suspects he is approaching the Great Moment when the pouring out of his life will be complete. How tender must this moment be for him! How healing to find a disciple who is bold with her love. How it must have pleased him to see someone who would not refuse the call even in the face of likely criticism.

Jesus' delight is obvious in his words to Simon. He praises this unknown woman and her dance of love. He points out to Simon that her love and faith have created a holy place in his spirit that will help him prepare for the great outpouring of his life.

What about you and the alabaster jar of your life? How do you live out your vocation to love? How do you break the seal that imprisons the treasures within your being? What dance of love will be yours today? Who will you anoint with the loving kindness of your presence?

Sitting in the morning shadows, the jar on my shelf brings many people to my mind and heart—people who have broken open the alabaster jar of their lives to anoint me. Fingering my

Jesus beads, I begin slowly to call out their names in prayer. One name for each bead! I move slowly through this procession of names, praying for each person, "Jesus, in the secret of her/his heart teach wisdom."

Each time we pour out the ointment of our lives, a healthy hollowing out takes place and we become more open. Our openness prepares us for the insight God desires to give us. That sacred space of openness becomes our wisdom school and Jesus rules the world from our hearts. The more we allow God to use us freely, the more translucent we become.

As you continue making the Word of God your home, pray that the Word will bring about a great freedom in you, so that your entire life will be a majestic liturgical dance, a dance of love.

Reflection and Prayer

- The woman with the alabaster jar is being drawn like a magnet to the one she loves. Are you able to find a part of your story in her story?

- Reflect on the alabaster jar of your life. What is the precious ointment you are being called to spill out for the life of this world? Of all the gospels you have meditated on throughout your life, which one has served to break open the alabaster jar of your heart?

- Who in your life is in most need of the presence of your anointing love?

Jesus, Lover of My Soul,

Now it is time for me to take the alabaster jar of my life and anoint the broken hearts and bodies of your people. Lead me on this journey of love. Show me where I must go. Reveal to me those persons who are in most need of your healing presence, that I may be for them what you would have me be: your own body, blessed, broken, and given for the life of this world. **Amen.**

6. Pilgrimage to the Heart of God

Prayerfully read Psalm 84.

Be attentive to your pilgrim-heart.

The late Paschal Botz has a book on the psalms titled *Runways to God*.

I have always loved that title and I love what Father Paschal says about praying the psalms.

"Runways to God" suggests rising with mind, heart, and body through prayer into the great realm of God. Not to give our whole self to the Godward thrust means dragging one's feet, clinging to things less than God. Flying and praying are far more arbitrary actions. "Reason and science govern the one, revelation and faith the other" (Preface ix).[4]

When I meditate on the psalms, I often think of them as "runways to God."

Psalm 84 is a pilgrim song. There is a pilgrim in each of us. We often sense the pilgrim aspect of our lives when we experience being stirred by a memory, a word, or a story. Something awakens our yearning for purposeful living. We are drawn into a deeper search. As we become more sensitive to such moments, we may become aware that our entire life is a pilgrimage. It is not always possible to ritualize our pilgrimage in the traditional way of actually traveling to a sacred site; however, we have within our beings a pilgrim path. Every time we prayerfully walk through a Scripture passage, we can make that prayer journey, a pilgrimage. The Word of God becomes our pilgrim guide. Each time we sit down at the altar of our own lives to evaluate our growth in Christ, whether this is through spiritual direction or part of our personal rule of life, we are on pilgrimage.

It is possible that this psalm was sung by pilgrims on the way to the temple in Jerusalem. Sometimes we are able to make a pilgrimage to a particular shrine, a cathedral, a temple, a holy mountain, even to our birthplace. But there are also inner pilgrimages we can make. All these pilgrimages are sacred. We move toward a place of deeper intimacy with God. We walk in the footsteps of other pilgrims who in their own unique ways *led the way.* Now it is our turn! We journey to our personal yet communal Zion. The "on the way" part of our journey is as precious as our arrival.

In using Psalm 84 for your personal prayer, note the rich imagery used. The psalmist describes this journey with deep emotion. Intense longing, trust, gratitude, hope, joy, and more pour forth from the psalmist's lips. Be attentive to the passionate tone in the psalmist's voice as you move contemplatively through the pathway of words.

As you are guided through the psalm, you will be encouraged to pause at personal pilgrim sites along your inner pathway. You are on the road to Zion. In biblical history, Zion usually refers to a certain section of Jerusalem. For your pilgrimage through this psalm, you might look at "Zion" as your own personal promised land, a place where God dwells. Or, it could be the temple of your own being where the Spirit of Jesus lives.

Here are some aids for your prayer "on the way" to Zion.

> *My soul is longing and yearning,*
> *is yearning for the courts of the Lord. (v. 3, Grail)*

Listen to the intense yearning in these words. Longing for God is a good prayer. Examine your heart in relation to your own desire for God. Are there exceptional moments in your life when your desire for spiritual growth is deeper than at other times? If so, what is going on in your life to stir up the longing in these special moments? After reflecting on those questions, spend some time prayerfully yearning for God.

> *The sparrow herself finds a home*
> *and the swallow a nest for her brood;*
> *she lays her young by your altars . . . (v. 4, Grail)*

Here is a nostalgic cry from the psalmist! Even the sparrows and swallows find homes in God's sanctuary, building nests for their young. Allow yourself to become a creature with wings. Fly like a bird to the altar of God. Lay your young dreams on the altar. Your hopes! Your desires! Your whole self! This is your second stop on your pilgrimage through this psalm. Remain here as long as you wish.

> *They walk with ever growing strength,*
> *They will see the God of gods in Zion. (v. 8, Grail)*

Reflect on your stepping stones of strength along the way. As you move forward on this blessed sojourn, name your experiences of growing stronger. Do you know that with God's help, you have the power to change your bitter valleys into springs of living water? If you are faithful to your inner pilgrimage to the promised land of God's heart, then you also can become a pilgrim site for others on the way. Name the wisdom experiences, both painful and joyful, that have brought you to this moment of refreshment. Name your teachers and guides.

> *One day within your courts*
> *is better than a thousand elsewhere. (v. 11, Grail)*

Every pilgrim faces obstacles on the pilgrimage. Where are the "elsewheres" of your life? What situations, people, or fears dampen your enthusiasm for reaching the inner courts, the dwelling place of God? What prevents your growing intimacy with the Source of your life? What stifles your healthy self-knowledge?

Describe a day you have spent in the courts of God. What was the environment of your life that made that possible?

> *For the Lord God is a rampart, a shield;*
> *he will give us his favor and glory. (v. 12, Grail)*

On your pilgrimage through daily life, can you recall times when you truly experienced God being your strength? A sun of warmth and growth! A shield of protection! Pray to be given an upright, honest heart as you continue to move from strength to strength on this happy pilgrimage.

Reflection and Prayer

- A pilgrimage can be as simple as moving from one church to another for a short visit. Or, keeping in mind that the whole earth is God's temple, you might travel from one nature sanctuary to another: a park, a botanical garden, a nature trail. Consider designing a simple pilgrimage for yourself.

- Create an inner pilgrimage made of sacred moments, experiences, and memories. Pause at each sacred event, remembering the grace of that moment.

- Choose one of your favorite gospels and use the pilgrim format to pray through the gospel. Try to be quite visual as you pray. Behold the people, images, and experiences that take place in the gospel. In your mind's eye, see the story unfolding as you read and pause at key events in the account. Allow it to unfold as though you are actually present.

O Pilgrim God,

You once led a people, dear to your heart, through the desert land of their exodus journey. Now I invite you on a pilgrim journey through the scenic and wilderness lands of my heart. Stop at the lovely shrines along the way. Enable me to see the beauty of many sacred places in my life. Together let us pray before the shrine that is me, created in your image. Show me my goodness and strength on the path that leads through the temple of my being. Pause also at the places where I am lost, deluded, and imprisoned in my own shallowness! Anoint those places with a glance of love. Transform all within me that yearns for renewal. Refresh what is stale. Open what is closed. Rekindle what has grown too dim to give light. O Pilgrim God, journey with me to the promised land of my own being. **Amen.**

7. The Prayer of Creation

Prayerfully read Psalm 148.

> *All things praise God by simply being themselves.*

This magnificent hymn of praise gives witness to the truth of these words. In ordinary moments of daily life when prayer and praise seem far from your lips, consider memorizing this psalm. Notice that the psalmist asks the moon, sun, and stars to praise the Lord. The mountains and hills, the snow and mist, the fire and hail—all are asked to praise God without ever speaking a word. From the heavens and from the earth praise is to ring forth. They are all drawn to the divine in wordless love.

If the fruit trees, the cedars, and even the hail are to give praise, then it follows that there is a way of praising God in which the spoken word is unnecessary. There is a Word that differs from the spoken kind. Sometimes it flows forth in the simple silence of *being* as shown in the mountains and hills. There is a Word that leaps up in the crackling of the fire; it rides in on the moaning of the wind and in the roar of the wild beast. Could this too be praise? Could all of creation be drawn like a magnet to the divine?

Perhaps we who depend so much on words that are spoken and written need to discover the art of praising God in the silent cathedral of our beings. We can learn from nature the art of praising God without words. I have noticed that when I spend more time with nature, I find it easier to praise God in this profoundly simple way.

Creation itself is a sacred text
through which the presence of God is revealed to us.
(Christine Valters Paintner)[5]

The earth keeps drawing me into greater awareness. Each new awareness increases my gratitude. The prayer of gratitude needs no words—only a heart open to what simply *is.* I arose early one morning, went outside to praise God, and lo! Everything was already offering praise. The God of the heavens and the earth was being blessed in the beautiful prayer of dawn.

The fresh, crisp smell of autumn moving over into winter was a prayer of praise. Even leftover sprigs of green grass were praying their way out of the brown crumbling leaves that had fallen to the ground. The sun writing its golden name in the skies was a prayer of praise. I looked around, and behold—everything was praising God through the simple act of being: the carpet of needles in the pine grove, the geese honking their way through the skies, the arms of the oak tree stretched out in a beautiful welcoming gesture, crumpled and brown leaves returning to the earth, feathers dropped by the Canada geese as they grazed for grass seeds, the squirrels gathering their nuts for winter, the pathways through the monastery park, the labyrinth with one sole walker. Everything, in its own way, was praising the Creator of heaven and earth. And thus it became clear to me; we need only to be attentive, to enter nature's contemplative prayer of praise.

All of this praise and prayer taking place in the midst of the humdrum places of daily life reminds me of my need to surrender some of my action. Learning to put down my tools of work becomes a blessing. Each of us needs to practice the art of *being* as opposed to *doing.* Go outside. Stand beside something that is already praising God. Let the sacredness of that prayer seep into your being. All that is drawn to God is drawing you with it. Let your great efforts fall away. Allow your little longings to arise. Keep company with the things of earth that pray without words. Look around you. There are prayers of praise everywhere. Be with the prayer you see. When you return to your work, you may be surprised to discover that some of this praise has slipped into your soul, making it possible for you to continue your work accompanied by a new song in the ground of your being.

At the end of Psalm 148, the kings of the earth, indeed, all the peoples of the earth—high and low, young and old—are summoned to give praise to the holy name of God. What might happen if the rulers of all nations would take seriously this request? What if, at the beginning of each new day, our rulers paid attention to the natural praise of the universe and allowed that prayer of praise to take root in their souls?

With your heart's eye try to envision the leaders and peoples of all nations standing, praising God, amid the rocks and the hills, the thorns and the blossoms, the desert sands and the morning star. If we were able to absorb this prayer of praise, could we ever again stand in the killing fields of war torn zones without the realization that something in our lives and on our planet is terribly out of focus?

Yet no matter how *out of focus* we might be, God has planted in each of our hearts *seeds of praise*. Perhaps it is time to plant them in our world and watch them blossom.

Reflection and Prayer

- What is your understanding of praise? What does it mean to you when we say that all of creation is praising God just by being?

- How is it possible for you to praise God without words?

- Practice living with creation for a day. Let this be a day of praising God.

- Spend time with something in creation: a tree, a rock, a garden, the sky, the earth, a blade of grass. Write a prayer or poem honoring the object of your praise.

O Tree of God—Tree of Life,

In the gift of your shade, I stand, my heart raised to your Creator. Your branches call me to reach out in all directions to many people. Your branches remind me of the sheltering arms of God. Your roots call me to be rooted in all that is good and nourishing. Your roots ask me to spend time in the ground of my being. Teach me, like you, to praise God in the silence of my being. Help me to surrender unnecessary words. Draw me, like a magnet, into the abiding love of God. And when it is time for me to die, teach me to die gracefully and joyfully. Teach me to let go as you let go of your leaves each autumn. In living and in dying, teach me to praise God by living well and dying well. **May it come to pass!**

8. Consecrate Them In Truth

Prayerfully read John 17:1-26.

We are all included in this touching prayer of Jesus.

This beautiful chapter in the Gospel of John is steeped in the language of a tender farewell. Aware that he must soon leave the ones he has loved and mentored, Jesus is pouring out his heart to the one he calls *Father.* The tone of his prayer is a loving angst regarding his beloved disciples. This passage is the high point of what is often known as "the last discourse," although no actual dialogue takes place. It is his last intimate plea on behalf of those he has begun to call friends. Listening to the deep emotions in Jesus' words, I found myself wondering about the nature of his prayer in those moments when he slipped away from the crowd for solitary prayer in the hills of Judea.

Looking toward the heavens, he prays for his disciples and for all who will come to know God through their words. We do not know where this great priestly prayer took place. Perhaps it was while praying in the temple, around a table after a meal, in one of his disciple's houses, or even out on a hillside. Of course it is the prayer itself, not the location, that is of importance to us. Picture yourself present in the mind and heart of Jesus at that moment. In the timelessness of eternity, place yourself in the company of Jesus and his disciples. Pray these words of the seventeenth chapter of John's gospel; then sit quietly and experience the wonder of being included in this beautiful farewell prayer.

An invitation to eternal life

Jesus asks to be given glory so that he may return glory to the one who sent him. What is glory? We speak the word often, sometimes casually. But have we thoughtfully considered the nature of glory? Brilliance! Shining Light! Luminosity! Radiance! Splendor! Beauty! All of these are words we might use to describe the brightness we call glory. It is a revelation of an inner quality that emanates from the source of one's being. The glory Jesus speaks of is a glory that he shared with God from all eternity. This glory he also shared with his disciples and now desires to share with all of us.

In his prayer Jesus has a sense of completeness about his work on earth. There is a *changing of the guard* mood here. Having completed his mission, he is bequeathing it to his disciples. His stance is one of loving concern for their welfare. This glorious gift will support them in more fully understanding who they are. The Source of all light has shone upon Jesus, and now he is asking for an abundance of that splendor to share with his disciples, so that the shining might continue when he is gone.

Jesus' prayer also embraces a desire to bestow eternal life on his disciples. And what is eternal life? *"Now this is eternal life, that they should know you, the only true God, and the one whom you sent, Jesus Christ"* (John 17:3). Eternal life is knowing Jesus. How can we experience eternal life through knowing Jesus? This is an important question. I encourage you to put it in the backpack of your soul and take it for a long, leisurely walk: eternal life is to know God and to know Jesus. The word *know* is one of deep intimacy in biblical language. This was the word used to describe the intimate love relationship between husband and wife. Keeping this in mind, then, reflect on your knowing God as union with God. This union is the eternal life that can begin here on earth. This is what Jesus was trying to teach his disciples. Recall the conversation Jesus had with his apostles in John 14:9. When Philip says, *"show us the Father,"* Jesus' answer clearly states that if his disciples know him, they also know the Father.

Jesus' remarks about eternal life and knowing God are a reminder that although we are disciples of Jesus, we ultimately belong to the one who created us. It is the spirit of Jesus who sanctifies us and shares with us divine life. Each of us is called to a deep union with God. That union is the beginning of eternal life.

> *Protect them with your name;*
> *consecrate them in truth. (see vv. 12, 17)*

As the prayer continues, we see that Jesus' desire for unity becomes fundamental. He longs for us to be one—united under the name of God. His request that we be protected with the name of God suggests that there is power in that name. God's name is a protective shield for us. We are to be anointed and guarded with the divine name. His desire is for us to be drawn to the divine.

Jesus is aware that his disciples will experience persecution. Thus in the spirit of the Lord's Prayer he asks that they be delivered from the evil one and be consecrated in truth. As we struggle daily to keep spiritual values alive, it would be a wonderful spiritual practice for us to turn our eyes toward heaven each morning. Then with eyes toward heaven, we ask that we be consecrated in truth—that we be surrounded and protected by God's Word, which is truth. The word *consecrate* is rich in meaning, suggestive of a life wholly surrendered—given over to good, to God.

The prayer ends with the promise of a perpetual indwelling presence. Jesus will continue to reveal God's name to us. Divine love will keep flowing from the Father to Jesus and from Jesus to us. It is heartening to know that the kind of union we will enjoy in heaven can begin here in the midst of our daily efforts to live the Christian life.

When I am discouraged, I often return to this prayer of Jesus. Remembering that he is also praying for me takes the edge off my discouragement. I too am a disciple of Jesus. I feel honored each time I meditate on this incredible chapter from the Gospel of John. Once again I am drawn like a magnet to the divine.

Reflection and Prayer

- Have you accomplished the work Jesus sent you to do? Have you even considered the truth that you too have been sent by God?

- Do you ever pray for those who may come to know the message of Jesus through your words, or because of the way you live out the Gospel?

- How do you feel about being a part of the glory of God? Do you find it consoling to know that you are a little spark from the Great Spark?

O Source of All Light,

I look to the heavens as I offer this prayer. How grateful I am that Jesus included me when he prayed for his disciples! In the spirit of the words of Jesus, I ask you to consecrate me in truth. Increase my love by helping me to remember that Jesus chose to share with me the glory you gave him. Reveal to me my own inner quality that flows from the Source of your glory. Support me in my desire to be faithful to the gift of your intimate presence. Gift me with Jesus' concern for others. Make us all one in our desire to be disciples of truth. Teach us to radiate your life wherever we go. I ask this in the name of Jesus. **Consecrate us in your truth!**

Poetic Summary of Chapter One

Drawn Like a Magnet

Each time you break open the Word of God you are invited to die a little. It is a dying that is full of living, a death that is life-giving. Unlock the door of your heart. Open the eyes of your soul. Allow yourself to be vulnerable to the hallowed words. These words will wound you even as they heal you. They will challenge you in the same moment they bless you. They summon you to move into the growing places. They call you to trust an invisible Source of life. They draw you, like a magnet, to the divine.

Don't be afraid of your death. When that time comes, "I will draw my breath and your soul will come to Me like a needle to a magnet."[6] In these revealingly mystical words, God speaks directly to the heart of Mechtild of Magdeburg. These words are also for you—whoever you may be—for the great death at the end of our lives is not the only death. There are little deaths along the way. Each death has the potential of drawing you into the Holy One. Your breath is not your own; it has been borrowed from God. Each breath draws you into greater intimacy with the divine.

If God has spoken to Mechtild in such beautiful, mystical language, rest assured this message is also for you. You too have the heart and soul of a mystic. On your pilgrim path through the hours of the day you will encounter many life-giving deaths. Each surrender is a little dying. Every act of love is full of life and death. Each covenant promise requires a bittersweet yielding of the will. Every leaning toward God is a little conversion in which you are drawn, like a magnet, to the divine.

You are being drawn! Between your first breath and your last breath the poem of your life unfolds. Every step is a dance step. The dance of birth! The dance of life! The dance of death! Surrender your need for certainty as you fall into your soul space. You will not know whether you have found life or death as you gaze into the face of God.

Chapter Two

The Deepening
Places

"Deep calls to deep," the psalmist prays (Ps 42:8). What is deep recognizes the depth of another. What is deep recalls a depth once known. There is a depth in us to which we must return. We came from God, the Source of all life, and we are returning to that Source.

In this chapter you will be praying with Scripture passages that encourage you to go deeper into the Holy Mystery. There is a depth within you that you have not yet discovered. Life in God is an adventure. You are encouraged to venture forth into the unknown. Learn to trust even the words you do not fully comprehend.

Stand as a pilgrim before these Scripture texts. Some of these words will bless and comfort you. Some will inspire you; others will challenge you. Be particularly attentive to words that create a movement in your soul. Be lovingly aware of words that pierce your heart. Trust them. Wait with them.

The poem "A Gap in the Cedar" by Roy Scheele illustrates how I am asking you to approach these sacred texts. In the poem, someone is standing by a window. You perceive this person to be pensive, perhaps even a bit sad. Suddenly there is a movement in the snow-filled branches of the cedar; the branches mysteriously part, and then swing back together. The poet contemplates the reality that in the short space of the opening and closing of the branches an experience of grace takes place. "Something went wide in me," he says.[1] At that moment the poet is deeply moved and you sense a return of peace, a lifting of the spirit.

Waiting before the window of Scripture is somewhat like this. At times you will experience "a widening of the heart." Something will stir within you. It may feel like a divine anointing. These heart-widening moments are vessels of opportunity. It is time to pause—time to wait.

Experiences such as these suggest a readiness for transformation—an invitation to go deeper. Trust these moments! Allow them to serve as a catalyst for opening your heart wider still. The Word of God is sometimes sent to you in exceptional ways, drawing you into the deepening places.

1. The Tapping of the Heart

Prayerfully read 1 Corinthians 2:1-16.

> *[W]e speak God's wisdom, mysterious, hidden,*
> *which God predetermined before the ages for our glory. (v. 7)*

God's wisdom is mysterious, Paul tells us. It is often secret and hidden. It catches us off guard, startling us when it comes unexpectedly—in both simple and profound ways. It is hidden in many places—in the human heart, in our first and last breaths, in the birth-cry of a baby, in the heart of a seed, in the opening of a bud, in the shining of the sun, in soft falling rain, in the power of a storm, in the turning of a leaf, in a change of heart, in the pages of history, in our daily crosses, in the cries of the poor, in a heart moved to compassion, in moments of forgiveness, in joy and in sorrow, in the pages of Scripture. It is hidden in Jesus crucified; in Oscar Romero shot down at the altar in El Salvador; in the five sisters from Ruma, Illinois, killed in Liberia—martyrs of love. It is hidden in the deepening places of your life, even in the places that are waiting for your arrival.

All of this suggests that the wisdom of God is not unreachable for us. Our God is a sharer of divine wisdom and the spirit that moved over the waters at creation is moving still. As we learn to live with expectant, listening hearts, we will be more receptive to this holy wisdom that often shows up on our doorstep when we are looking for it in the heavens.

In every age, in every nation, in every people God's wisdom has been revealed. Revealed, but not fully perceived or received. It takes a special kind of person to grasp this mysterious wisdom that comes to us from the Spirit. Mindfulness, desire, and vigilance are gifts that can assist us in grasping the wisdom of God that surrounds us and abides within us.

In his book *The Heart of the Hunter*,[2] Laurens van der Post tells his story of living in the Kalahari Desert with the bushmen of South Africa. It became obvious to van der Post that these primitive peoples knew intimately the presence of wisdom in every blade of grass and in every heartbeat. The bushmen had a mysterious kind of inner knowing. They knew when the enemy was approaching and danger was near. They knew when to move their camps, and when and where the rains would come. They knew where to go for the hunting that would sustain their lives. When questioned about this mysterious inner knowledge, they spoke of what they called the "tapping of the heart."

From an early age, they had been commanded to heed this tapping. When they felt it coming, they were to become very quiet inside and to listen vigilantly to the tapping. It was like a sixth sense, an unexplainable knowing. Reflecting on the uncomplicated lives of these ancient peoples, I have come to believe that this mysterious knowing in them was nothing less than the wisdom of God.

Are our lives, rooted in Christ, any different? What is this mysterious hidden wisdom that Paul speaks about in his first letter to the Corinthians? We are told that we have the mind of Christ. We have a mystical, compelling presence within—the Spirit of Jesus dwelling in the depths of our beings. Surely, we too can learn to attend the tapping of the heart, which is the wisdom of God revealing itself to us in the deepening places of our lives. To catch up with this wisdom, we must learn to listen with a simplicity of heart that is difficult for most twenty-first-century people. In order to understand this hidden wisdom of God, we need to learn how to connect with the part of us that is most primitive, or, we might say, the part within us that is most original—closest to the Source of all life.

This wisdom often shows its face in the voices and lives of the lowly, in the lives of the little ones whom the world is slow to defend, in Christ crucified today. Blocked by a thousand noises, this wisdom is difficult for the world to hear. But to you who have the mind and heart of Christ, to you who have felt the magnetic presence of God drawing you, listen: *listen to the tapping throughout the land*, hear the tapping of the unborn who are not allowed to be, the tapping of prisoners who need rehabilitation and forgiveness more than punishment, the tapping of the human masses who cannot afford healthcare. Hear the tapping of the homeless, the unemployed, those dying alone and forgotten, immigrants who long for a better way of life, children who have never known a day without war, and the elderly no longer considered useful to society. Indeed, hear the tapping of anyone who feels the painful burden of exclusion.

Listen to the tapping! Listen to the breath of the risen Christ, breathing you ever more deeply into your divine heart-space. For when you become one with Christ, it will be easier to hear the tapping of your heart. To hear the tapping "out there," you must become silent enough to hear the tapping "within."

Recently I have added to my daily practice of "deep listening," a touch to my heart-space when words, events, or experiences take hold of me in a significant manner. For example, in reading a book, if I am moved by a specific sentence or paragraph, I pause and put my hand over my heart. I also do this when I am watching TV or a movie—the program continues but the symbol of my hand on my heart tells me I don't want to forget that image or those words. At those times when I am in conversation with someone and what we are trying to convey to one another seems vital, my hand over my heart reminds me not to take this moment of communion lightly. Often during Eucharist when specific passages or moments anoint me, my hand automatically goes to my heart. The more frequently I practice this kind of presence, it becomes, for me, a way of listening to the tapping of the heart. This simple ritual enables me to believe in and treasure the deepening places.

Hold dear the truth that the Spirit who knows the depths of God also knows your depths. In that secret place within, the wisdom of God is hidden. Ponder this mystery as you listen to the tapping of your heart. There are sorrows in our families, our communities, and the world at large that might be alleviated if more people would learn to listen and respond to the wisdom of God alive and well in their hearts. Learn to believe with an extravagant conviction in the deepening places of your life. Never forget, there is a depth in you that you have not yet fully discovered. It waits for you!

Reflection and Prayer

- Ponder the various ways you have heard the tapping of the heart. During the coming week, practice listening to "the tapping."

- How would your life, and those with whom you live and work, be transformed if you really believed that you have the mind of Christ?

- Take some time to pray about and claim your own mysterious and often hidden wisdom.

- Rent the movie *A Far-Off Place*, based on a book by Laurens van der Post. Carefully watch and learn from the bushman Xhobbo in the movie.

Holy Wisdom of God,

You are hidden in our hearts. Hasten the day when our sorrows will be eased because we have dared to believe in and act on the truth that we have the mind of Christ. May the power of the spirit of Jesus totally envelop our being, deepening and perfecting the wisdom you desire to share with us. Teach us to listen with attentive ears to the *tapping of the heart*. **Amen.**

2. Staying Connected to the Vine

Prayerfully read John 15:1-8.

> *Remain in me, as I remain in you.*
> *Just as a branch cannot bear fruit on its own*
> *unless it remains on the vine,*
> *so neither can you unless you remain in me. (v. 4)*

"I am the vine, you are the branches" is a well-loved and frequently quoted text from the Gospel of John. Having grown up in the vineyards of Arkansas, this Scripture passage has special meaning for me. As symbols often do, it suggests a veiled intimacy between us and God.

Jesus often used symbols from the world of nature as teaching tools. He encouraged his followers to look at the common things around them: bread, water, salt, light, fig trees, birds, sheep, rocks, seed, wildflowers, mountains, vines, and branches. They were to learn lessons from these natural gifts by listening to their wordless sermons. These teachers from nature were intended to lead Jesus' followers into a deeper relationship with God.

Perhaps you too have discovered a beautiful truth in these "nature teachings" of Jesus. In the ordinary miracles of nature there is a thin veil that separates us from the face of God, or, we might say, a cloud that obscures us from the divine mystery. Jesus often gives us clues, trying to lead us closer to our sacred Source. He wants to help us break through the veil that separates us from our heart's deepest longing, which, of course, is union with the divine. The Christian Celtic peoples spoke of these elusive connections with God as the *thin places.* In this description, they were suggesting that one need only lift a gossamer-like curtain to behold the face of God. Let's try to imagine now that we are the branches growing out of a mystic vine.

I am the vine, you are the branches. (v. 5)

This beautiful vine and branches passage reads like a poem. Poetry is the language of the soul. It is frequently used by those on the spiritual journey. A poem is a means of depicting the beauty of certain truths by using words to help create images that lead us into prayerful reflection. In Jesus' poem about the vine and the branches, we are reminded that just as the branch cannot bear fruit unless it is connected to the vine, our lives will not be fruitful if we are separated from Jesus, the vine. It is possible to live in separation from the vine even though we are not living in serious sin. There is the unease of living with indifference or apathy, which is a spiritual disease. Perhaps we are lukewarm in our relationship to God and others, and therefore pruning must happen in our lives. Maybe we need to prune away certain attitudes concerning other members of the branches. It is a grace to be able to recognize how the branches of our lives need to be trimmed. The trimming is generally for our good and for the good of the faith community of which we are a part. The pruning will assist us in our journey to the "deepening places." It is a work of transformation that will enable us to discover the incredible beauty of the intimate bond we have with Christ.

Remain in me, as I remain in you. (v. 4)

Use your imagination as you listen to the voice of Jesus speaking these words to you. Notice that the words are both an invitation and a promise. We are invited to abide in Christ; we hear also his promise to abide in us. The way we are to stay connected to the sacred vine is to live in such a manner that the words of Jesus come true in us. How, then, are we to live so that Jesus remains the fundamental core of our lives? The answer to this question is both simple and difficult. It requires the work of a disciple. A disciple is a disciplined listener. We will become better listeners, and thus better disciples, if we learn to romance the Word of God.

As you read the words of Scriptures, linger with them. Repeat the words. Memorize them. Write them on your heart. Sing them. Contemplate them. Abide in the Word of God. Remain in the Word. Prune away the obstacles that weaken your communion with God.

When I was young, I used to walk beside my father when he was pruning the grape branches. In cutting away old, dead wood, he was awakening the energy sleeping in the wood. As that energy came to life, it would initiate a new season of growth. Even fruitful branches are trimmed so that they may bear more fruit.

Pause now to reflect on the dead wood of your life that needs
to be pruned away
so that you may be refreshed and enlivened
on your journey to the deepening places.

The invitation of Jesus, "Remain in me, as I remain in you," is, in reality, a lovely prayer that can be prayed in different ways: live on in me as I live on in you. Abide in me as I abide in you. Stay rooted in me as I stay rooted in you. Imagine Jesus praying that prayer to you. Hear the longing in his voice, longing for connection, for an enduring relationship. It is an echo of his own union with the Beloved. He desires that same union with you.

It is an invitation to each of us to enter deeply into communion with the divine. These words point to the heart of our baptismal call of union with Christ.

Our efforts to stay connected to Christ will help us to remain spiritually linked to one another. It is not possible to be united to Christ without being united to the larger Body of Christ. We are lying to ourselves if we believe that we are connected to the vine of Christ while living in hostility with any of the branches. Living out of harmony with one another prevents us from bearing fruit. The more we can learn from each other and support one another's respective journeys, the greater will be our intimacy with the One to whom we all belong.

Reflection and Prayer

- Read John 15:1-8 again with a heart longing to stay connected to the vine. Let these words follow you throughout this week: *Remain in me! Live on in me! Abide in me!*

- Can you recall moments when you had a felt-sense of living in Christ, of being connected to the vine?

- Why do you think deeper communion occurs at specific times in your life? Does your life seem more fruitful at these times?

- Do you remember fruitless seasons when nothing seemed to grow? What circumstances or events in your life tend to draw you away from recognizing and remembering God's indwelling presence?

Jesus, Vine of God,

Just as you have proclaimed to be the vine, I proclaim that I am one of your branches. To abide in you, to remain rooted and connected to you, is my soul's dream. My heart desires you. O Vine of God, protect and cherish all your branches. Prune me carefully so that you may never cut away more than I can bear. May your pruning be only to awaken the sleeping life in me! May all that is weary and bored be snipped away so that my very best self can arise! Prune away the dead wood from my life. Awaken me to my full potential. **Amen.**

3. Clothing Yourself with Virtues

Prayerfully read Colossians 3:1-17.

For you have died, and your life is hidden with Christ in God.
(v. 3)

To be hidden with Christ in God is to experience a mystical death. The culmination of this kind of death is actually a passing into God while we are yet alive on this earth. We are able to experience union with God because we have allowed the ego to fall away. Too much "I" in our lives is detrimental to the possibility of union with God. Paul asks us to trade the deceptions of the vices for the truths of the virtues.

Put on then, as God's chosen ones, holy and beloved, heartfelt
compassion, kindness, humility, gentleness, and patience. (v. 12)

We live in a world where much time is spent on the adornment of the body. Department stores are filled with clothing, jewelry, cosmetics, perfumes, colognes, potions and lotions of many varieties and prices—all with the promise of making us beautiful. Do you ever wonder why people spend so much time and effort trying to cover over every wrinkle and blemish of the skin? And do their many efforts really bring them closer to the true desires of their hearts; are they finding the peace and self-esteem for which they are seeking? There is certainly nothing wrong in wanting to look beautiful. Yet as we strive to *look* beautiful, perhaps, we need to encourage one another to practice *being* beautiful. The Scriptures tell us that the hidden character of the heart, expressed in the imperishable beauty of a gentle and calm spirit, is the adornment that is precious in God's sight (1 Pet 3:3-4). In receiving these insightful words, may we be inspired to decorate our bodies in memory of the One in whose image we are created.

Our desire for outer adornment may subconsciously be symbolic of another kind of beauty for which our hearts hunger. Paul understood the human heart and was well aware of our hidden hunger for holiness. We are encouraged to put aside all obstacles to this holiness. Take time to meditate on the things with which you adorn your body. Do you see a connection between outer and inner adornment? The concept of clothing, adorning, dressing, is one of intimacy. This is the language Paul uses when he asks us to remember who we are: "God's chosen ones, holy and beloved." We are encouraged to clothe ourselves with the virtues, enfolding them all with love.

When Paul asks us to set our hearts on things above, he is not telling us to despise the things of this earth. He wants us to cast off the things that are not working in our lives. If we begin to place the emphasis on our desire for God, which is surely our deepest hunger, then our secondary hungers will become healthier, enabling us to make better choices about the things that are not working for our good. It is about understanding and setting priorities. When our desire for outer beauty marries our desire for inner beauty, integration will take place in our lives and we will be standing on the edge of transformation. We will be drawn into the deepening places.

The advice given to us in this text from Colossians reminds me of one of our former community customs. When I was a young sister, we were given a specific prayer to pray for each piece of clothing we put on in the morning. We called these "dressing prayers." Although we no longer use these prayers, they served as an excellent reminder of the holiness of our bodies and the need to put on Christ each day. They helped us to stay focused in the present moment. Since we knew these prayers by memory, the morning dressing ritual became a natural part of our day's beginning. For example, while putting on our religious habit we prayed, *"Through your grace, dear Lord, I wear this holy dress; grant that I may be entirely changed in you as I love and serve you in peace of heart."*

Reflecting on this old monastic custom, I have adapted it and created a spiritual practice for dressing myself with the virtues. Although this is not something I do each morning, I often use this ritual for special seasons like Advent or Lent. Symbolically I practice putting on the virtues. It is a daily challenge to clothe myself with mercy, kindness, humility, gentleness, patience, peace, and gratitude.

I recommend this practice to you. Take gratitude, for example. How might you clothe yourself with *gratitude*? What prayer could you allow to flow out of your heart as you symbolically put on this virtue some morning? How about *kindness* and *patience*? As you dress yourself with these virtues, think of creative ways to ritualize them with gestures or words. Create your own "dressing prayer" for each virtue. Unlike clothing in the department stores, this apparel never goes out of style. It is always in season.

As I write this reflection, I am sitting in a garden park watching the trees undress themselves for the winter. The once green leaves of their spring and summer wardrobe are falling all around me, returning to the earth—a choreographed farewell. Just as the trees of autumn clothe themselves with emptiness and trust, surrendering leaves that are no longer needed, may we too be able to surrender all that detains us from putting on Christ.

May we be able to live lives hidden with Christ in God!

Reflection and Prayer

- During these next weeks, would you be willing to make Colossians 3:12-17 a spiritual practice? In the morning consciously choose one of the virtues to practice throughout the day. Clothe yourself with mercy, kindness, humility, gentleness, patience, peace, or gratitude. Let this be your morning prayer.

- Call to mind other virtues that are not mentioned here. Add them to your list.

- Of all these virtues, which one are you most in need of at this time in your life? Invite it to breakfast. Keep company with it throughout the day.

O You Who Adorn the Earth with Beauty,

Clothe me with your image. Just as you robe the meadows and fields with wildflowers and grain, so too take special care in adorning me each day. When I awaken from sleep, clothe me with the dawning light. Embellish me with patience and compassion. Beautify me with gentleness and humility. Remind me to put on the virtues you have planted in my being. Let these be my robes of glory as I go forth, in faith, to meet the day with a willing spirit. And over all these virtues, enfold me in love. Encircle me with the spirit of all that is noble, gracious, and wise. **Clothe me with your Beauty!**

4. The Comfort of Being Known by God

Prayerfully read Psalm 139.

> *O Ancient Love—Oldest Ancestor of my Soul,*
> *your love for me has been revealed in the deep recesses of my being*
> *and I will never be afraid of being known by you again.*

Psalm 139 reads a bit like a love poem. It is a psalm of revelation. The personal love flowing from the created to the Creator and likewise flowing from the Creator to the created is revealed. The one reciting the poem becomes intimately aware of this mutual exchange of love.

Surely we have all experienced a lingering longing to be deeply known. Although we yearn to be known by God or some cherished human being, there is also a tendency in us to fear being known so intimately. This kind of knowing requires an unfathomable trust that isn't always easy to unearth in our often guarded human hearts. Thus we sometimes move back and forth between a desire for the comfort of being known by God and a fear of being known so deeply. We aren't quite sure if we can trust this deepening place that the saints have called friendship with God. Scripture supports this truth in countless ways; nevertheless, some of us feel a reluctance to call God our home. To acknowledge that the deep-rooted angst in our lives has anything to do with spiritual matters is difficult for many people.

As you reflect on this well-loved psalm, perceive it as a prayer of intimacy. It is an affirmation of God's steadfast, loving presence in our lives. Tread lightly on this path of words. They are words that proclaim the truth of a loving union with God. Take time to reflect on how you really feel about God leading you into the deepening places of your life. How do you feel about God knowing you so completely?

> LORD, *you have probed me, you know me. (v. 1)*

How many of us have taken the truth of these compelling words into the depths of our being? To be so utterly and intimately known by God could be a source of great peace. As I reflect on this psalm more closely, however, I become keenly aware that this intimate knowing of God causes me to experience feelings of both security and caution. I want to go to what I call the *deepening places* but I hesitate, somewhat fearful about what might be asked of me when I get there. How much probing can I handle? My ultimate reluctance is that I will be asked to change some of my comfortable ways of living.

Do I want to be known so thoroughly? Is this in-depth kind of knowing a comfort to me? Am I at home in those divine hands? Does the eye of God resting on me cause me to feel protected and safe? Or, do I feel exposed? Do I allow God's penetrating gaze and careful probing to frighten me? Am I unsure of God's intent?

And so, with a little caution I continue to pray, "*you have probed me, you know me . . .* " The word *probe* invokes certain images. I think of a small object inserted into something to test its condition. Probing suggests a penetrating search. In this case it is a search by the Beloved for the beloved.

This psalm evokes an image of a delightful and radical Presence following us through our days. Someone has suggested that you pray this psalm daily for one month as a way to cultivate a sense of God's intimate presence in your life. I encourage you, though, not to look at God's probing as a judgmental kind of prying into your personal life. Instead, think of it as a loving interest akin to Jesus' gaze into the heart of the woman at the well (John 4). Jesus probed into her life but it was a gesture of love. That encounter transformed her into a disciple. As each of us becomes willing to experience the truth of this psalm, we too will be changed ever more radically into disciples of love.

> *My travels and my rest you mark;*
> *with all my ways you are familiar. (v. 3)*

Many of us struggle with the difficulty of knowing ourselves; thus it can be a comfort to rest in the truth that there is someone who is lovingly familiar with all our ways yet not bent out of shape. The lamplight of God's eye shines upon our sins and weaknesses, our sorrows and despair, our fears, our joys, our anger, our dreams, our love, our heart's yearnings. All is known. Nothing is hidden. A change sometimes occurs in our lives when we are able to accept God's knowing gaze. Slowly, the "knowing of God" begins to console us rather than frighten us.

> *You formed my inmost being;*
> *you knit me in my mother's womb. (v. 13)*

This image comes to mind: an age-old woman sitting in the chapel of some anonymous womb lovingly knitting a human person into being. How beautifully separate each of us has been designed. How unique! A work of art! An original! Not another like us! There are times, though, when this solitary nature of ours makes us lonely. It is the loneliness of that lost memory of being fashioned in secret and in love. It is the loneliness of trying to discover and remember who I am and where I came from. It is the loneliness of the holy mystery of being known by a God I cannot see. It is the loneliness of recognizing that if I am to make the journey to the deepening places, I must be willing to be known. In meditating on all these things I arrive at the dear truth that loneliness is an ally, a support, not a foe.

> *Probe me, God, know my heart;*
> *try me, know my concerns. (v. 23)*

We come back to the probing but this time we actually ask God to probe us. A conversion has taken place in our deep being and we are more willing to be known by God. A sweet handing over, better known as surrender, has replaced the fear. We don't seem to mind being tried in the fires of daily living. We even ask God to try us. My will and God's will have become one. I rejoice now in the comfort of being known by the Holy Mystery.

Reflection and Prayer

- Spend some time this week just dwelling in the intimacy of being known by God. Walk in the mystery of One who knows you well and loves you as you are.

- Choose specific verses from Psalm 139 to memorize.

- As much as we fear being known, there is nothing freer in our lives than opening our heart to someone we can trust. Is there such a person in your life?

Oh God, You Have Created Me and You Know Me,

Take away my fear of being known by you. Widen the doorway of my heart. You, who knit me together in my mother's womb, continue loving me into new ways of being. Reveal to me the beauty and goodness of my life. Encourage me to focus on my positive qualities so they will have a chance to grow even stronger in the womb of my acceptance. Lay your hand on my heart when I am tempted to nest on the negative pieces of my life. O you who fashioned my life, if the truth be known, it is not you before whom I tremble in fear. I am not nearly so afraid of you knowing me as I am fearful of coming to know myself. Replace my fear with love. Replace my reluctance to love myself with acceptance of your love for me. I am grateful for your knowing presence in my life. **May it grow stronger day by day!**

5. When Revelation Dawns

Prayerfully read Acts 9:1-19.

*A great turning happens in the human heart
when we are summoned
and we find ourselves leaning toward the voice that invites.*

Although we often speak of the conversion of St. Paul, if we look more closely at this story, we will note that Paul's encounter with Jesus on the road to Damascus is, in reality, a vocation call. In Galatians 1:15 Paul acknowledges that he was called by the grace of God and set apart before birth so that he might receive the revelation of Jesus and become an apostle to the Gentiles. Paul's assertion that he was called before birth is reminiscent of the call of two other prophets. *"The Lord called me from birth,"* Isaiah says in 49:1, and of Jeremiah, Yahweh proclaims, *"Before I formed you in the womb I knew you"* (Jer 1:5).

The poet David Whyte suggests that when revelation dawns in your life, you can never hide your voice again. You become impelled to speak the truth revealed. Certainly this was true of Paul. When Christ was revealed to him in that powerful encounter on the road to Damascus, he was transformed. He didn't embrace a new religion. He embraced the risen Christ. In that embrace, he became one with Christ. After Jesus captured his heart, all that passion went into teaching *the way* of Jesus rather than persecuting *the way*. Paul's entire ministry could be summed up in these few words from Galatians 2:20: *"I live, no longer I, but Christ lives in me."*

It is apropos that Paul should speak so intimately about his relationship with Jesus. There was a time when he had seen Christianity as a betrayal of Judaism. In his passionate intent to uphold the traditions of Judaism, he had persecuted the followers of Jesus. His encounter on the road to Damascus redirected that passion. Jesus spoke clearly and with authority: *"I am Jesus, whom you are persecuting,"* but Paul wasn't persecuting Jesus. That event was over. Paul was persecuting the followers of Jesus yet the voice said, *"I am Jesus, whom you are persecuting."* These are truth-telling words. Take them to your heart and listen deeply to the spaces between the words. These words suggest that Jesus identifies with us so completely that if we are wronged in any way, he is also wronged. Likewise if we do harm to any of his disciples, we are harming him.

Is the passion of Saul alive in you? Do you live with the passion of Paul? Or perhaps you are somewhere between Saul and Paul. It is likely that Paul lived in between for awhile also. Conversion happens in the spaces between events. When we are meditating on the Word of God, we hear God's call somewhere in the spaces between the words. That is why pausing for reflection is so important.

Each of us needs to hear the call again. It is easy to walk *the way* with little excitement, with a minimal amount of delight. It is easy to grow used to being Christian. The church is a bit like a big pot of soup. It needs to be stirred up once in a while or it will get stuck on the bottom. What is stuck on the bottom is nourishing for no one.

So let's open our hearts again to God's call. Is there anything in you that needs to be stirred up so you can hear the call anew? What would need to change in your life for you to be able to say with Paul, "It is not my life I am living; it is Christ who is living in me"? After Paul's encounter with Jesus, he got up from the ground with open eyes but couldn't see. How many of us walk around with open eyes yet fail to see? To see the deep truths, more than our eyes must be open. Sometimes we, like Paul, have to grope for a hand in the dark and allow ourselves to be led like a child. Learning to trust is crucial.

For three days Paul, under the guidance of Ananias, was without sight and neither ate nor drank. During those days I suspect Paul did eat, but the food was different from what we ordinarily hunger for. He had been led to the *deepening places*. He was learning to trust in new ways. He was being fed from within. He had tasted the sorrow and joy of transformation. The voice he heard on the road to Damascus still echoed in his soul. He was being emptied of himself, and thus set free. It was a freedom he had never experienced. He had to taste that freedom in the darkness of trust rather than light of sight. What about you? Who have been catalysts for you in restoring or improving your spiritual eyesight? What is your last memory of God working in you with such power that, although you might not have seen a light from heaven, you knew without a doubt you were being touched by grace? Do you ever have a sense that God has called you before your birth? Have you ever experienced God's revelation in your life so poignantly that you knew you could never hide your voice again?

These questions are not part of a test. There is no need to answer them in order to get a satisfactory grade. There is no need to answer them at all; but there is a need to pray them. As the German poet Rilke suggests, we may one day, all unexpectedly, just live our way into the answer. These are good questions and praying with questions can be healthy for the soul. I suspect, though, that you will not live your way into the answers unless you take them to your heart for careful consideration, which is part of what prayer is all about. Careful consideration about our life with God! Careful consideration about our pilgrimage to the deepening places!

Reflection and Prayer

- Use Paul's vocation story to ponder and pray the moments of revelation in your life. You too have been called and set apart by grace. Stir up your memory of moments when you have been claimed by Christ. Name some of your callings, your invitations to grace. Linger with them and be blessed.

- Take the questions from the second to last paragraph of this reflection and use them for your prayer.

- What kind of disciple are you? Is there anything you would need to change in your life in order to be able to say with conviction, "It is not my life I am living; it is Christ who is living in me"?

- Write your own vocation story.

Surprising and Dynamic God,

You break into my life in unexpected ways: a personal stormy moment, a field of wildflowers, a cup of tea with a friend, a special book, a prayer with someone who is discouraged, a Sunday morning Eucharist, a leaf falling from a tree, an interruption, a surprising insight. You call me into the sacred circle of life. You clothe me with Christ-Power.

You called me before my birth. You opened my eyes and my heart to moments of revelation. Set free in me any resistance to being your disciple. May I never hide my voice again! **Amen.**

6. A Space of Love

Prayerfully read Genesis 18:1-15.

Offer hospitality also to the stranger who lives in your own heart.

The account of Abraham and the divine visitors has been beautifully portrayed by artists throughout the ages. View this story as you would a painting. See it in your mind's eye. Sitting by his tent in the heat of the day, Abraham sees three strangers standing nearby. He hastens to greet them. He not only invites them to stay awhile and rest in the shade of the trees but he also asks to be allowed to serve them.

We can be fairly certain that Abraham did not recognize these strangers as divine visitors. He had no inkling of the joyful announcement of Isaac's birth, which would soon be foretold. He was merely performing the accustomed hospitality and respect that one in his day would show to strangers. In the harsh, barren land of Abraham's environment there were no locks for the doors and hospitality was a necessity rather than an option.

When friends arrive in our lives, it may be easy to invite them in and put the teakettle on; however, opening one's home and heart to a total stranger is a gesture of admirable trust. In biblical days the host and the guest bonded with one another and became kin even if the guest was a stranger.

In our times, hospitality is not quite as simple as it was in the Arabian Desert. Our world is violent and fearful. We are often afraid to open our door or to pick up a stranger on the highway and this is certainly understandable. Yet if we could open our hearts to the stranger, believing that somewhere in that person is a goodness and loneliness that longs to be known, we would be living in the kind of world most of us dream about. When we reach out in compassion and love to other people, we are filling the space that surrounds them and us with love. We are creating a space of love. We are rooting ourselves in love and hospitality.

An icon depicting Abraham and the divine visitors hangs in my office. It is there to remind me that each person who passes through my door comes with a blessing. If I look at my guest as an intrusion rather than a revelation, I am unable to receive the blessing.

In their book *Gifts of the Spirit*, Philip Zaleski and Paul Kaufman share a Bedouin greeting to a guest:

> *O Guest of ours, though you have come, though you have visited us, and though you have honored our dwellings; we verily are the real guests, and you are Lord of this house.*[3]

This greeting suggests that when someone comes to us in need, he or she turns us into the guest by giving us the opportunity to create a space of love.

The way we greet someone mirrors how we are living. In ages past when lives were lived more simply, little prayerful greetings were common. Today you would probably startle someone if you should greet them with, "The Lord be with you" or "May God dwell in your coming and your going." Yet such greetings suggest an awareness of the sacredness of the person you are meeting. The Hindus use the greeting *Namaste*, which roughly means "what is divine in me recognizes and greets what is divine in you." For Christians that might be "the Christ in me greets the Christ in you."

Reflecting on these greetings, I recall Jacob's greeting to Esau when they finally meet face-to-face after a period of estrangement over that "stolen blessing" (Gen 27). The meeting is filled with forgiveness and Jacob's words to Esau are so tender they deserve our remembrance: *"to come into your presence is for me like coming into the presence of God, now that you have received me so kindly"* (Gen 33:10).

In his Rule for monastics St. Benedict spotlights his conviction that when we come into another's presence, we are in the presence of Christ when he says, *"All guests who present themselves are to be welcomed as Christ"* (RB 53.1).[4] The more we journey into those *deepening places* of our lives, spending time there in prayer and creating a space of love, the more ready we become to treat all we meet as we would treat Christ.

Hospitality is about having open hearts, not just open doors. Using words from 1 Thessalonians and 1 Peter, St. Benedict encourages us to make hospitality a way of life. *"Your way of acting should be different from the world's way; the love of Christ must come before all else. . . . Never give a hollow greeting of peace or turn away when someone needs your love"* (RB 4.20-21, 25-26).

The strangers who came to Abraham and Sarah's tent did not receive a hollow greeting of peace. They were given not only the shade of the trees of Mamre but also the shade of a loving presence. In the space of love that was created they received what God wants to give us every day, through one another: a blessing!

Reflection and Prayer

- Imagine yourself as a guesthouse. When is it most difficult for you to keep the door of your guesthouse open?

- What opportunities were given to you today to practice hospitality?

- Can you recall a time when an interruption in your life turned out to be a blessing?

Oh Welcoming One,

You are my guesthouse, my hermitage, my dwelling place. Your hospitable spirit frees me from my nagging fears of not being accepted. In my deepest moments of estrangement from myself and others I discover my home in you. There is no lock on your door. You are all openness. Inspire me to be a guesthouse for others. Take the lock off the door of my heart. I long to be a space of love for everyone! I yearn to be a place where all can be at peace and feel at home. May the interruptions of my day become pathways of love instead of annoying disruptions! Give me a welcoming heart. Make of me your guesthouse. **Amen.**

7. Opening Your Heart to Guidance

Prayerfully read Psalm 25.

> *Unbar your heart and simply wait for God.*
> *There is so much grace in waiting.*

Before immersing yourself in the words of this meditation, obey the words above. Slowly and with reverent attention read this psalm in its entirety. Read it with long silences in between the sentences. If you do this, you will be praying the psalm rather than just reading it. This prayerful and careful gleaning of the Scriptures is the way of *lectio divina*, the process you are using as you are drawn more deeply into this continuing romance with the Word of God. Above all, I encourage you to move slowly. The best kind of romance is not hurried.

> *To you, O Lord, I lift up my soul.*
> *I trust you, let me not be disappointed . . . (vv. 1-2, Grail)*

The beginning of the psalm lends itself beautifully to movement and gestures. Repeat the first line, raising your hands in prayer. Lifting up your soul suggests a moment of prayerful union with God. On the other hand, lifting up your soul might seem rather nebulous. How exactly do you lift up your soul? Your soul is the fundamental nature of who you are, the very essence of you—what we believe will remain alive, even after your body passes away. Thus "lifting up your soul" doesn't necessarily require gestures. It could be an inner turning to what is in you that you believe to be eternal. It may be getting in touch with your spark of divinity. We tend to live rather distracted lives; thus the inner turning toward the soul is an excellent spiritual practice.

If we desire to move into a deeper relationship with God, it is essential that we live with unguarded hearts. Thomas Merton once suggested that the most dangerous person in the world is the one who is guided by no one. Psalm 25 is a prayer for guidance. In the first seven verses we see a person who is utterly open to know God's ways, one who is ready and willing to be guided. The psalmist also exemplifies a willingness to wait.

Openness! Readiness! Patience! Spend a little time reflecting on those qualities in your life. How do you experience being open to *guidance*? Who are your teachers on the spiritual path? How is this *readiness* to go deeper into God's ways visible in the way you live? How do you feel about *waiting* for God to make known the paths you should walk? How do you feel about waiting for anything? Do these words of the psalmist, *"For you I wait all the long day"* (v. 5), ring true of your life? How important has a teacher or guide been for you? Pause for a few moments and pray for the teachers in your life. Or if need be, pray that God will lead you to someone who can become a mentor for you.

In order to go deeper into our interior life and be molded by the Source of all life, it is important that we learn the art of creative waiting. This kind of waiting does not suggest that we sit inertly on the sidelines and do nothing; however, neither does it encourage us to try to do everything on our own. Creative waiting is a deep listening that is at the heart of all discernment.

The second part of the psalm, verses eight through fifteen, is a prayer of praise for God's goodness in your life. Although you have asked God to clear up the haze on your path and reveal the way you must walk, the words are hardly out of your mouth when you are drawn to remember the many ways you have already experienced divine guidance. Your life has been enriched liberally with blessings. Pause now and give names to the blessings that encircle you each day. Let gratitude make its home in you as you remain focused on the One who protects you.

The psalmist prays, *"The Lord's friendship is for those who revere him; to them he reveals his covenant"* (v. 14, Grail). Again we return to the theme of guidance. Counsel is a form of teaching. A covenant is a bonding relationship with God. This covenant, in itself, can be your teacher. Remember your baptismal covenant—a pledge of friendship and love. Sit at the feet of your own promises. Renew your covenant with God. Write a mission statement for your life. Who are you in relationship to God? How do you experience this bonding with the Holy One? Are there new promises you feel called to make with the Beloved? Have you been able to keep alive the reverential awe and childlike wonder you once possessed? Are you able to delight in the presence of God?

In the third and final section of the psalm, a mood of desolation descends upon the psalmist. Since this has become your prayer and you have taken on the ambience of the psalmist, make every effort to feel what the psalmist is feeling. Permit yourself to cry out to God for comfort. You have prayed for guidance. You have acknowledged God's attentive presence on your pathway. However, the human condition is frail. Your mood has changed, and once again you find yourself acknowledging your need for mercy and consolation.

In mentioning your foes (v. 19) you might want to think of these enemies as interior blocks to spiritual growth. What is it that keeps you trapped in your troubles? Why has this loneliness descended on you again? What is the source of the affliction that you feel? Why is it so difficult for you to enter the deepening places of spiritual growth with ease? Provocative questions can revitalize your prayer. They serve as therapeutic guides to your heart's uncertainties. They help you get in touch with your feelings. Nowhere are feelings expressed more honestly than in the psalms. Mature prayer nudges us all toward honesty.

Return to the beginning now and pray the psalm again. More than likely it will have a greater significance for you when you pray it a second time. Throughout this week, contemplate your *openness*, your *readiness*, your *patience*, and your *trust* in divine goodness, as you offer the Holy One the troubles of your heart.

In completing your reflection on Psalm 25 create in your mind's eye the following icon: "You are putting your impatience into the heart of God." Sit for awhile with that image.

Reflection and Prayer

- Are you comfortable in using gestures in your personal prayer? How would you describe the action of lifting up your soul to God?

- In Psalm 25 we have looked at waiting as a spiritual practice. What are your experiences of waiting for God?

- Many questions have been asked in this reflection. Go back through the pages and underline the questions. Sit with them meditatively. Ask your own questions. Let the questions be your guides.

- Who were your teachers throughout your earlier years? Who are your teachers and guides today?

You, O God, Are My Counselor,

I am lifting up my soul to you. I am handing over my questioning heart. All is in your keeping. Give me good questions to ask and worthwhile things for which to wait. Teach me to wait creatively, with patience, believing that you will lead me on the pathways I must walk. Open my eyes so that I may notice that my paths are strewn with blessings. How tenderly you have guided me throughout my years, even when I walked in darkness.

May the bond between us deepen! May the covenant of age-old love between us be renewed! I sit at the feet of all my old promises, asking you to help me remember my desire for you. Bring back the childlike wonder I once possessed and teach it to feel at home in my adult life. I am open. I am ready. I am not yet patient. I am putting my impatience into your heart, O God. Receive it. Transform it. **Amen.**

8. Every Day Is the "Day of the Lord"

Prayerfully read 1 Thessalonians 5:1-26.

> *For each of us there is a "day of the Lord"*
> *when God breaks into our lives unexpectedly.*

This *breaking in of God* does not have to be a frightening experience. It can be an awakening moment, and perhaps a deepening experience.

For the moment, however, let's take a look at what the phrase *Day of the Lord* has meant to our biblical ancestors. When this expression is used, it ordinarily points to events that are to take place at some unknown time when God intervenes in history to achieve and complete the divine plan for human beings. It is a day of cleansing and purification. The language centered around the Day of the Lord is often full of frightening visions and bizarre images; thus it is understandable that for many people it has become a day of dread. (See Isaiah 7:18-25; Amos 5:18-20; Joel 1:15-18.)

In the New Testament the Day of the Lord is often equated with the second coming of Christ and understood to be a moment of judgment. Jesus emphatically tells us that no one knows when this day will be. What we are told, however, is that it will be sudden. It will come when we are not expecting it. For this reason we are asked to be vigilant. Be attentive! Attentive living is to be your focus as you pray with Paul's first letter to the Thessalonians.

If you are to live so as to be always ready for the coming of the Lord, you will need a watchful heart. Vigilant living is a beautiful prayer that can become a path of life for you. It is a way of pure prayer. As you strive for attentive living, try to envision the Day of the Lord as an event that takes place in some small way each day. Every day God breaks into your living. How might your life change if you practiced believing in God's coming? What if at the end of the day you glanced back through the hours, naming moments of God's visitation? If you could live with such vigilance, you might begin to take a fresh look at the Day of the Lord.

In this Scripture text Paul is talking to us as believers, so he reminds us that we are children of the light and of the day. This reminder can be medicinal. We need encouraging prompts to help us carry on. Remember, then, that you are not walking in darkness. Open your eyes. The path you walk is flooded with light. You do not have to go to some mountain and wait for the Second Coming as some have done. Your goal is simply to live in the light—live as one awakened. Your homework is to be vigilant, sober, lucid, and aware. Watch for daily visitations from God. Anticipate all the blessings that take place each day rather than dreading things that may never happen. Each morning practice believing that your mind will be filled with amazing insights. A positive attitude can assist us in shaping our days.

Paul encourages us to clothe ourselves with the garments of faith, hope, and love. So let us put on the robes of light. Let us dress ourselves as people who are ready for the bright journey of each new day, remembering always that the bottom line is not God's wrath; it is our salvation. God desires us, longs for us. Both in death and in life it is the Holy One to whom we belong.

If we all belong to this unseen God, then we also belong to one another.

We are to give over our hearts into one another's keeping, supporting each other and building one another up in love. How can our lives not deepen if we strive to live with this kind of presence?

This is the great coming of God—that moment when we are caught up in awareness of who we are and whose we are. The true Day of the Lord will dawn when we are able to say an enthusiastic yes to living in union with Christ. This radical communion with Christ will enable us to light one another's paths so that we need never walk in darkness.

In bringing his teachings to a close Paul pleads with us to respect those who are in authority over us. To Paul's request for respect we might add the responsibility to pray for our teachers. Those attempting to guide us are often as imperfect as we are and so even if, at times, they lose our respect, may they never lose our prayers, for as St. Jane Francis de Chantal reminds us, *"We are all capable of each other's faults."*

As for Paul's final words of counsel, each of us would do well to inscribe them on our hearts, so let us pray:

> *May the God of peace sanctify us so that we may learn how*
> *to live together in harmony!*
> *May our patience and loving support of one another be so obvious*
> *that our lives overflow with gratitude!*
> *May we joyfully nurture the Spirit's flame that burns*
> *in every heart!*

Reflection and Prayer

- Would you like to live more vigilantly? What might you add to your daily practice of prayer to make this possible?

- At the end of this day make a list of God's visitations. You may be surprised at how many times God broke into your life today.

- Later this week find a companion to pray this Scripture passage with again. Become pilgrims moving through this path of words, together yet alone. At the end of your pilgrimage share with one another the pilgrim sites where each of you paused for deeper reflection.

O Lord of Deepening Experiences,

Open my eyes to the many ways you visit me each day. Do not let me sleepwalk through the hours of the day. Teach me vigilance. Robe me with hope and anticipation as I begin each new day. I do not want your coming to be a frightening experience. Let it be instead a gracious deepening within my spirit. Break into my living with your gracious presence. Startle me into lucidity! Amaze me with grace! Give me pilgrim feet on my path through the hours of each day. Increase my awareness that every day is the "day of the Lord" and because of our growing intimacy, I need never be afraid. **Amen.**

Poetic Summary of Chapter Two

Listen to the Deepening Places

Learn to listen! The voice inviting you is voiceless. Most ancient of all voices! Enticing voice without words! Listen from within the cells of your being. From the marrow of your bones, listen. From the deepest source of your life, listen. A holy vibration, a gentle movement, a persistent tugging—summons you into the deepening places.

Learn to go deep! Like waves of the sea you are being pulled back into the depth. Embrace the depths! *Deep calls unto Deep!* There is a depth in you to which you must return. Most silent of all calls! A voice without words calls you to the deepening places.

Learn to abide! Remain in Christ as Christ remains in you. Be like a sponge. Soak up the Word of God. Absorb it. Make the Word your home. Live in the Word! Abide! Dwell! Inhabit! Reside! Trust the deepening places.

Learn to be silent! Silent as the leaves that fall, silent as the blossoming flowers, silent as the moment before dawn! You are being summoned into the temple of silence. Practice silence, for this voiceless voice can be heard only in the shrine of silence. You are being chosen for the deepening places.

Chapter Three

The Beautiful Struggle of Daily Life

Beauty and struggle are not ordinarily seen as kindred spirits. In the midst of the struggle, it is usually difficult to see beauty. Our ability to look back and reflect on some of the discouraging ordeals from our past enables us to understand that those experiences were not totally devoid of blessings. We may even begin to understand something of the sacramentality of our daily lives. With eyes of faith, we are able to rename the struggle, and honor the hidden life. When we take these daily struggles to the kiln of our hearts for reflection and prayer, we are often able to find the gold in the struggle.

The scriptural reflections in this chapter salute the sacred struggle that goes on constantly in our daily lives. Hopefully we will be able to find the grace that rises out of every crisis. These Scripture texts reveal to us the extraordinary boldness of the disciples of Jesus and prophets of God.

Open the windows to both your past and present experiences as you pray with the Scripture passages offered to you in this chapter. You will probably be able to find your own life in the pages of Scripture. The Word of God and the word of your daily life experiences will be your guides as you pray with the beautiful struggle of daily life.

1. Being Loved through the "Meanwhiles"

Prayerfully read Matthew 14:22-33.

> *Meanwhile the boat, already a few miles offshore,*
> *was being tossed about by the waves,*
> *for the wind was against it. (v. 24)*

The account of Jesus walking on the water comes immediately after the feeding of the five thousand in the gospels of both Matthew and Mark. For your reflection, consider this opening scene. It has been a full day of ministry: teaching and healing, feeding the multitude. Toward the end of the day Jesus is weary. Feeling a need to be alone, he sends his disciples on ahead of him to the other side of the Sea of Galilee. In doing this, whether it was his intent or not, Jesus makes a statement about how important it is to integrate prayer and work.

It may not always be possible for us to spend time alone in prayer at the end of our work day; and even if we are able to find some space for solitude, we cannot be assured that the struggles of daily life will suddenly cease. It is, however, a healthy practice for us to attempt to place ourselves in the "white space" of those in-between times so that we make room for Christ's presence, both in the calm and in the storms of life. Jesus often comes to us in these in-between times, in the "meanwhiles" of daily life.

> *Meanwhile the boat . . . [is] being tossed about . . . (v. 24)*

Meanwhile the mortgage is due, the roof is leaking, and you've heard rumors of cutbacks at work. *Meanwhile* the person you love most is drinking too much, one of your children is in trouble, and you're wondering if it's your fault. *Meanwhile* God seems to have gone to the Bahamas, your faith is crumbling, and your brother was just diagnosed with cancer. *Meanwhile* your spouse is criticizing you, the baby is crying, and the doorbell is ringing. *Meanwhile* you are three days late for a deadline assignment, a telephone call requests that you come to the hospital, and the car won't start.

All these situations suggest some sort of storm in our lives. The waters are raging! Your personal storm may not have been mentioned but if you pick up pen and paper, I am reasonably sure you will have no difficulty naming your storms. These storms have a way of distracting us from the Divine Presence that is always accessible to us. Thus we may find ourselves questioning, where is the Christ who once walked across the waters? Why are we sometimes able to experience Christ moving over the turbulent sea of life toward us while at other times there seems to be a great absence of the Divine Presence?

Each of you will have your own answer to those questions. My answer is, in some small way, connected to a daily faithfulness in prayer. It is a massive challenge for me to go off to the mountain to pray when I think I don't have time. When my prayer life suffers, my ability to trust God during the storms of life also suffers. If I wait until I think *I have time*, I will never slip off to the quiet places. Thus, when the storms arrive, I look out through the turbulence and see only the ghost of God. Isn't this what happened to Jesus' disciples as they battled the waves of the sea? Jesus was coming to them across the waters but they became fearful, thinking they were seeing a ghost. They didn't recognize Christ just as I don't always recognize Divine Presence in my life. Finally, it was the voice of Jesus that brought them to their senses and restored some semblance of peace. My life is not so very different. I too must learn how to listen for the voice that awakens me to the One who surfs the storms with me.

The voice of Jesus in the midst of the storm

"Take courage, it is I; do not be afraid" (v. 27). Is this not the voice we all long to hear in the storms of life? These words of Jesus are like an echo from the past, a wake on the waters of life. We may not hear them verbally but somewhere in the marrow of our bones we sense a gracious presence that faithfully surrounds us. A presence that is wholeheartedly for us! God's promise of faithfulness to us is present in both the Hebrew and the Christian Scriptures. Every time we are commissioned to a new ministry, that same promise follows us or goes before us, like our shadow. The words may differ but the promise of presence pervades.

As you find yourself battling the tempests of daily life, choose one of these encouraging promises as a prayer to follow you through the storm as you, like Peter, walk across the waters to meet Jesus. Listen to God's voice throughout the ages:

Take courage, it is I; do not be afraid. (Matt 14:27)
I will be with you. (Exod 3:12)
When you pass through the water, I will be with you. (Isa 43:2)
Fear not, for I am with you. (Isa 43:5)
I am with you to deliver you. (Jer 1:8)
I will make your name great, so that you will be a blessing.
(Gen 12:2)

We do not know if the prophets and disciples of God heard these promises in audible words or if they sensed them in the marrow of their bones. What I am trying to highlight for you is that they believed in a sacred presence that was somehow hidden in their own presence. Their belief gave them the strength to trust and to walk through their fears with courage.

Jumping into the water

There are times in my life when I am overpoweringly moved by the memory of the voice of Jesus in the gospels. Delighting in the encouraging voice of the Beloved, I am ready to jump into the raging waters of daily life. However, like Peter, my focus can so easily turn from the positive to the negative. I am tempted to dwell on the illusion that God really isn't with me. I am tempted to dwell on the illusion that I am all alone. When I am obsessed with my human limitations, I become afraid. I lose faith in what I once believed I could do. I forget the Gracious Presence that surrounds me. I forget about the One who is wholeheartedly for me, standing up inside me, oar in hand, ready to row if necessary. When I forget, I become paralyzed by fear.

How different my life is when I remember to wrap my days around the voice of Jesus, allowing the echo of this gospel passage to keep sounding in my ear: "Take courage, it is I; do not be afraid."

I am still trying to discern how to be who I say I am—a Benedictine, a vowed monastic living my life around a Rule and the Gospel. Recently, my personal prayer has been given over to praying the Rule in light of my own faithfulness to it. What I am discovering each day is that the Gospel really is Good News. No matter what my daily struggle may be, when I struggle in the heart of a gospel, it becomes a beautiful struggle. Perhaps that is the essence of the Gospel—the beautiful struggle of daily life!

Reflection and Prayer

- Name a few of the storms in your life. How have you remembered God's promise of presence during the stormy times?

- Are you sometimes able to slip into one of the quiet places when the waters rage?

- When was the last time you, metaphorically speaking, experienced the Divine Presence standing up inside you?

- What does the voice of Jesus sound like to you?

O Christ of Our Fears and Our Courage,

When you see us tossed about in the strong winds of life, come to us walking over the stormy waters. Climb into our boats and help us row. We need a sense of your presence to do even the difficult things of life; but to do the impossible, we need to feel you standing up inside us. When the headwinds of life catch us off guard, refresh our memory of your enduring presence in our lives. Remind us to keep our eyes on you and the gifts you have so generously bestowed on us. In the midst of our fears, show us our courage. In the heart of our doubts, give us a glimpse of our faith. In the midst of raging waters, become our living water. Teach us to trust that you are still walking across the water trying to catch our eye. Help us to keep our eyes on you. **Amen.**

2. Opening Your Eyes

Prayerfully read Luke 24:13-32.

> *[B]ut their eyes were prevented from recognizing him. (v. 16)*
> *With that their eyes were opened and they recognized him. (v. 31)*

Praying with this familiar passage from the Gospel of Luke, I became aware of two very different experiences that can occur in my life. One is a moment of blindness—I do not recognize a movement of grace that is unfolding before me. The other experience is a moment of recognition—a veil lifts and I am in awe of the miracle before me. These two moments may often be the same experience.

As I recall the disciples' walk to Emmaus when Jesus joined them along the way, I am jolted by these words: *"but their eyes were prevented from recognizing him."* These were intimate friends of Jesus. They had shared much with him before his death. How could they not recognize him? Had resurrection changed him that much? Or was it death that had changed him?

As I questioned the disciples' unseeing eyes and hearts, I was given a glimpse of my own obtuse spirit and began to realize just how much I share their blindness. In this world so full of Christ, so full of blessings, so full of things for which to be grateful, how often I focus on the evil that surrounds me rather than the good! How often I allow the moment of sacramentality to pass me by! How often I moan and groan about something that has been taken away from me, failing to notice that I am utterly surrounded with gifts given. So often I do not see what is at my side, in my midst, in my heart! Sometimes it is a person that I fail to see. Sometimes it is the power of an experience that could be a healing force in my life if I would look at it with new eyes and allow it to be a moment of grace. There is much that I miss because I'm not present with authenticity. My body is there but my mind is distracted. Thus I miss the time of grace. I am very much like the disciples on the road to Emmaus. My companions on the road are numerous. They walk beside me like invisible blessings. They are vessels overflowing with gifts. Yet so often I miss the gift of the person in my midst. I forget to look into his eyes. I forget to invite her into my space. I keep rushing through my days. Something prevents me from recognizing the very ones who share my daily life. I miss the Christ figure standing beside me.

What is it that blocks my heart? What prevents me from seeing? What are the obstacles in my life that serve to extinguish my moments of recognition? As I pray with these questions, I realize that the blockage in my life has many faces. On some days my inability to see clearly comes from my preoccupation with my own agenda. At other times it may be my insecurity or my self-righteousness. The obstacle may be there because of a deep sadness or an unresolved loss. Whatever the cause of the obstacle, I know that healing can happen when I become open enough to pray with the root cause of my failure to see.

The second and more positive experience on my spiritual journey is the moment of recognition. It is present, as it was for the disciples, when my heart is softened through listening to someone who is on the road with me. I am able to see that person as a companion on the journey—a companion with experiences of interest to me and with wisdom for which I long.

The disciples who walked along with Jesus did not have closed hearts. Perhaps they were so full of sorrow that it was their grief preventing them from knowing him. Their hearts were obviously touched by this stranger who walked with them. Gradually, a new openness made its way into their hearts. They invited him to eat with them. When he broke the bread and handed it to them, *"their eyes were opened and they recognized him"* (v. 31).

I am grateful that this recognition took place around a table while sharing a meal. Amazing things can happen when we meet around a table. Miracles take place when we begin to feed each other. Barriers fall away. Eyes open. We see Jesus and one another in a new way and with a deeper insight. Moments of recognition can heal. It happened to the disciples. It happens to me. It has probably happened to you.

Reflection and Prayer

- Find a table, a loaf of bread, a few honest friends.
- As you break bread with one another, talk about the two moments discussed in this reflection. Share your moments of blindness and recognition—unseeing and seeing.

O Christ of the Emmaus Journey,

Stay with us in the evening of our lives. Come to our table. The bread we break is the bread of your presence. It is the daily bread of our life experiences, lifted out of each day's beautiful struggle. It is the bread of compassion and joy, sorrow and courage. As we gaze into the bread of our own lives, we begin to realize it is you who have been journeying with us all our days. Stay with us as our daily companion. In moments of doubt, as well as moments of deep and enduring faith, companion us on this journey. It is because of you that we keep on rising to new life. Rise with us! **Amen.**

3. Hold All Things Lightly

Prayerfully read Matthew 19:16-22.

What do I still lack? (v. 20)

In each of the Synoptic Gospels, we find the story of the rich young man who longed to follow Jesus yet walked away sad because of his many possessions. For the other versions of this story, see Mark 10:15-22 and Luke 18:17-22.

This gospel story has had a dynamic impact in my spiritual life over the years. It has pursued me, lingering longer than I sometimes wished. It is a gospel that won't go away. Because of its persistence in my life, I have spent a lot of time praying about its presence and pondering just what truths it wants to reveal to me. When a Scripture passage insists on following you through life, I suggest looking at it with x-ray eyes. Perhaps there is a message hidden in its shadow. Maybe God wants to speak to you through this story. Sometimes you have to become your own private detective searching for clues.

What does it mean to leave all and follow Christ? Why did the rich young man walk away sad? In praying with this gospel I am beginning to realize that I sometimes focus too exclusively on detachment. I have spent a number of spiritual seasons trying to rid myself of things because I believed God was calling me to a greater renunciation. Thus my efforts to free myself of clutter became another obsession. Getting rid of things became one more idol. I began to pray the following questions. Is all of this downsizing drawing me closer to God? Am I becoming a kinder, more compassionate person as a result of letting go of specific things? Does my presence to others have a greater quality? Is the simplicity I am striving for true simplicity? Or is it just more of my ego being exposed? Has simplicity enabled me to be more grateful for the gifts that I have? Finally, I returned to the rich young man's gospel question and asked, What do I still lack? The answers to these questions were a revelatory shock.

One day, during my prayer, the Spirit offered me a new meaning for this gospel. What if, rather than asking me to surrender everything, Jesus might be asking me to hold all things lightly? Is it possible to enjoy the gifts life lavishes on me without becoming obsessively attached to them? My possessions! My cherished beliefs, opinions, and ideas! My friends! My customary way of doing things! It occurred to me that perhaps I was being asked to loosen my grip just a bit. Holding things lightly does not require a total surrender, although it does imply that my hands and heart are open if this kind of surrender should prove to be the greater good. I began to hear an invitation to treasure all possessions, allowing them to become pathways to God. A new desire was born in me and I began to pray for the art of letting things go without obsessing about the process.

Every gift I possess can be an icon: an image of God, leading me to hallowed places. In her book *Penguins and Golden Calves*,[1] Madeleine L'Engle uses the phrase "a window to God" to describe an icon. I like that image very much. Everything I possess can be a window to God. However, to truly see my possessions as icons and allow them to bless me, I must hold them lightly. When I tighten my grip or cling to any gift in an exclusive kind of way, it becomes an idol instead of an icon. I have spent a good deal of my life juggling icons and idols. If I hold an object or possession lightly, it can become a pathway to God; if I cling to it tightly, it may become a stumbling block on my pathway to God. Since I have begun to look at detachment in a healthier way, the desire to surrender what is not assisting me on my path of spiritual growth has not gone away. The gospel story of the rich young man still attracts me. Something moves in my heart each time I read it. For this reason, I realize that I need to continually attend the truth of this gospel.

Now that my heart has opened wider to the recurrent transforming power of the Word of God, I am so much more aware that my first leaning toward what I believe to be God's truth for me may not be the final word at all. The invitation to deep listening never goes away. An important aspect of all discernment is to listen again and again—and to listen with others.

Reflection and Prayer

• As you continue to romance this Word, pray about your own icons and idols.

• What are the gospels (or other Scriptures) that won't go away in your life?

O Gift Giving God,

This I know to be true—all is gift. In your hands you hold age-old gifts that continue to flow into my life. Each gift bears the image of the giver. As I reach for these gifts, instill in me an awareness of the love with which you give. Inspire me to share with others the treasures you have poured into my life, for only then will your gift be a gift—when it is given away. Teach me how to give and how to give away, how to receive and how to surrender. Reveal to me both my icons and my idols. May I learn to live with open hands and open heart! **Amen.**

4. Everyone Needs a Refuge

Prayerfully read Psalm 16.

Keep me safe, O God; in you I take refuge. (v. 1)

We all need a refuge, a place to go when the storms of life rage, when uncertainty and anxiety become our roommates, when sorrows sweep through our houses, when the world around us seems to be falling apart. We need a safe place to go. In this place of refuge we pause to breathe in the midst of the storms. We practice remembering who we are. We remember our spiritual selves and the God to whom we turn in times of trouble.

The forest, meadows, and cornfield were places of refuge for me as a child. They were stations of solitude where I could sit and dream. They were places of healing where I could meander when I needed to wonder about things. In these beautiful places nature worked her medicinal miracles in me. I didn't know why I felt better in those places. Now, as an adult I am more aware of the healing properties of nature. The forest and the cornfields gave me companionship. The intimacy of the trees and cornstalks was like a little embrace. The meadow, on the other hand, gave me space and freedom. There are times when one does not want to be closed in. The sweet roaming grace of the meadow is a great metaphor for one who needs the freedom of not being bound. I no longer have easy access to cornfields, but I still occasionally seek out a forest or meadow. Trees will always be a refuge for me. The Word of God is written in their branches and in the spaces between the leaves.

Sometimes people can be a refuge for us. They are the wise ones to whom we flee in times of trouble. My mother was such a refuge. Just being in the shadow of her presence was a sheltering harbor for me. She has now joined the ranks of the communion of saints; thus I no longer enjoy her tangible presence, though sometimes I take refuge in memories.

Perhaps you too can remember special people and places to which you turned for respite from the storms of life. Although we will always need the comfort that comes from wise people and the medicine of nature, as we mature in our faith life, hopefully we will discover that ultimately God is our safe refuge. This is what the psalmist is proclaiming in Psalm 16. God is the sustaining presence that is our inheritance, our greatest good, our refuge in times of trouble. When we court other gods, the troubles in our lives tend to increase.

They multiply their sorrows who court other gods. (v. 4)

Who among us has never experienced the temptation to court other gods? These other gods may be anything from the things we own and the pleasures we seek to the work we do. Perhaps the most dangerous god of all is clinging to our own wills. And could it be that all the false gods we cling to are, in reality, our feeble attempts to find the living God? How easy it is to seek God in the wrong places! Yet we who proclaim that God is everywhere must examine even what seems to be the wrong places.

Perhaps someday we will wake up and realize that it was always God we were looking for. It was always God whom we wanted to be our refuge. Then in the face of this healing discovery, we will know experimentally that our sorrows only increase when we flee to other gods.

We live in a world beset by scandals. Jesus' request that we love our enemies seems only a dim echo locked in the pages of

Scripture. Consequently, we live in a world of war. Our hearts are saddened because of the scandal of child abuse, both in the church and in the world at large. When the abuse is brought about by religious persons, a sacred trust is broken. Thus we have the added temptation to make despair and bitterness our refuge. In times of violence and betrayal, where do we go for refuge? When peace seems an impossible goal, if you faithfully search, you may find a little harbor of hope in reach. Despair is never a refuge, though sometimes we are tempted to abide there. Bitterness is an empty song, a dirge of discord. The despair it gives birth to is not the path of life God wants to show us.

Life, with all its faces, is our inheritance. This is the life I encourage you to embrace, enhance, renew, protect, and cherish. Thus when those moments arrive when everything seems to be falling apart, when all the romance has gone out of our lives and we are left holding a handful of disillusionments, let us open the pages of Scripture. Perhaps we can take refuge in the wisdom of God's Word.

Reflection and Prayer

- Where do you go for refuge in times of trouble?
- What are the other *gods* that you sometimes find yourself courting?
- Do you agree with the suggestion that even when you look in the wrong places, you are ultimately searching for God?

O God, My Refuge, My Path of Life Forever,

This I know to be true—when I needed a refuge, it was always you for whom I was seeking! Every time I tried to fill my emptiness with too many things, too much food, too many words, too much work, it was always you for whom I was seeking. Every time I hoarded more than I needed, it was you for whom I was hungering. Every time I searched in the wrong places, I was searching for you. Every time I wanted to be right more than I wanted the truth, it was you for whom I was yearning. It was always you! You are my path of life. It was always you to whom I wanted to flee for refuge. **May my refuge be in you!**

5. The Power In Powerlessness

Read 2 Corinthians 12:1-10.

> *My grace is sufficient for you,*
> *for power is made perfect in weakness. (v. 9)*

These words are the *heart* of what Paul wants us to know in this twelfth chapter of his second letter to the Corinthians.

There was a time when Paul's boasting annoyed me, yet as I listen to his words with the ear of my heart I sense that he is breaking open his own heart as he shares his weakness with us. He is allowing himself to be vulnerable in speaking to us of Christ's power and his weakness.

There appears to have been a group in Corinth who was questioning the authority of Paul (2 Cor 11:1-6) and boasting of their superior credentials. Evidently they were boasting of their visions and using this to endorse their authority. Thus Paul feels called to boast about his own qualifications. In doing so, however, he makes it clear that his credentials come from his powerlessness, not his power. The power of God working through the weak vessel of his life is the gift he has to offer. Is this not the gift that each of us has to offer?

Visions, revelations, apparitions are a part of the Christian tradition. This is not the ordinary way that God speaks to us. Yet many saints tell of the Lord speaking to them in visions; our biblical tradition is rich with stories of visions and revelations.

The angel of God appeared to Moses in a burning bush (Exod 3:2). Jacob struggles through the night with a divine being (Gen 32); and "during the night" when a revelation of the Lord was uncommon and visions infrequent, young Samuel hears the voice of the Lord calling to him (1 Sam 3:1-14). Jesus is transfigured before the disciples; his countenance changes into glory and he is seen conversing with Moses and Elijah (Matt 17:1-8).

On the road to Damascus Saul has a life-changing experience when he is surrounded by a flash of light and hears the voice of Jesus (Acts 9:1-19). Could this be the experience Paul is describing in our reflection for today? As with many visions, we do not know if a physical being was seen, or whether the vision was imaginative or intellectual. We know only what Paul tells us. He was caught up in ecstasy, transported to another realm of being, and there he had a mysterious encounter with God. This mystical experience that took hold of him was not something he could satisfactorily share with others. He clearly states that he doesn't know whether this was an *out-of-body* experience. God knows, he says, and that seems to be enough for him.

All prayer is an encounter with God. Each time we approach God with faith and humility, believing that in some way we will be transformed, it will happen. If we come with willing spirits, and live for awhile in Christ's presence, our hearts will be pierced with love. The transformation may be ever so small; we may not be carried up to paradise, but if we come into that Presence longing for union, we will be touched by grace.

All we have to bring to our prayer is the small vessel of our lives. It is in the midst of that frailty that we are touched by grace. All we have to boast of is God's power in us. When we can admit our powerlessness, we won't get in God's way. We won't be our own obstacle. Those who are weak know they need grace. So, like Paul, we can boast of our weakness, for it is that very littleness owned that enables God to work in us and through us. Perhaps no one knows this as well as those who have worked 12-step programs in Alcoholics Anonymous. By admitting their powerlessness, they find a Higher Power. This is what Paul means when he says, "for when I am weak, then I am strong," which is another way of saying, "I live, no longer I, but Christ lives in me" (2 Cor 12:10; Gal 2:20).

When we become too sure of our own power, we often experience the "thorn in our side" that Paul speaks of—the thorn that keeps us humble. We don't know what that thorn was for Paul. Scholars speculate on various things. From our own living, however, we know what it is to struggle with intellectual pride, grandiosity, lust, greed, or perhaps some physical handicap or illness. When these painful obstacles to growth lead us to acknowledge our need for God, they end up working for our good. Until that happens, though, we may find ourselves asking God to lift this burden from us. It is then, if we learn to listen well, that we will hear God's voice saying, "My grace is sufficient for you, for power is made perfect in weakness." Our weakness, if owned, makes God's power in us available and visible.

Reflection and Prayer

- Stand in memory of one of your moments of vulnerability. How did that moment become a teacher for you? What did you learn? If you were not able to experience God's presence in that moment of pain, have you been able to look back now and recognize God waiting in the shadow of your pain?

- In the first step of the twelve steps of Alcoholics Anonymous we confess that our lives are unmanageable. It is difficult for many of us to acknowledge the vulnerability of not always being able to manage things on our own. Does needing help sound like weakness to you? Who manages your life? Does God need your help?

O You Whose Grace Is Enough for Me,

In my powerlessness I do not always find your grace waiting on my doorstep. I have to search with the wide-open eyes of a faith that sometimes seems to be missing. O hidden God, gift me with a wisdom that enables me to embrace my powerlessness as I search for its hidden grace. Strengthen me and give me the courage to ask my own weakness to teach me. Enable me to understand how even my weakness can become a path for spiritual growth.

In the midst of my vulnerability reveal to me just how much courage and strength I really have. You have not come to me in visions of glory, O God. I have seen you most often in ordinary ways and sometimes in the midst of weakness and confusion. Yet, in faith, I have truly seen you so I too will boast of your wondrous work in me. **May your work in me continue!**

6. Called to Be Holy

Prayerfully read 1 Peter 1:13-25.

> *[A]s he who called you is holy,*
> *be holy yourselves in every aspect of your conduct,*
> *for it is written, "Be holy because I [am] holy." (v. 15)*

Our call to holiness is, in reality, a call to obedience. The word obedience comes from the Latin *obaudiens*, which means "to bend the ear" or "to listen intently." We bend an ear to the divine sounds in our lives so that we might be able to discern how God is leaning toward us, listening to us. Thus the first call is to listen. We have here a lovely icon of the divine and the human listening to each other. Imprint that image on your mind!

And to what do we listen? God listens to the longings of the human heart. We listen to an innate and ancient call to become holy. We listen to our desire to be the person God is calling us to be, in Christ. Our faithfulness to this listening is the beginning of holiness. When we look at holiness in this way, it is easy to see that holiness is a process. For human beings this involves a journey not so unlike the exodus journey of the Hebrew people. That memorial journey, exodus, involved a moving away from slavery into freedom.

When we hear the call *to become holy "in every aspect of [our] conduct,"* it is easy to understand that such a command cannot be realized in a moment. Although we have been created in God's image, to live in that image requires a lifetime of faithful practice. Obedient listening becomes a way of life for us and it is important for us to believe that God is also listening to us. We are called to the daily task of reverently taking our lives into our hands.

I have used the phrase "taking our lives into our hands" intentionally, to suggest that holiness is not some kind of magic that takes place with our wishful thinking or even because our life is in God's hands. Holiness is not just something God does in us. It is a way of life that needs our cooperation. By listening with a spirit of obedience, we collaborate with the One who is already listening to our desire for holiness. It is as though, in some mysterious way, we are listening to God's longing for us.

> *[C]onduct yourselves with reverence during the time*
> *of your sojourning. (v. 17)*

Our sojourn on this earth can pull us in many directions. On the one hand, we live in a place of immense beauty and bright opportunities. We feel the tug of some invisible, creative force nudging us to take our place in the world of things. On the other hand, something also seems to be pulling us off track, away from our heart's most desired objectives. Although Peter tells us we have been ransomed from the futile conduct of our ancestors, we don't always experience the joy or completion of that ransom. The futile behavior still roams around in our lives. The indifference and even shallowness that we often see in the world can also be found in the mini-world of our own hearts. All of this causes confusion and sometimes camouflages the reverence that waits quietly within. Reverence is a well-chosen word in describing how we ought to conduct ourselves while sojourning in this pilgrim land. We are called to live in loving awe of the Mystery we name God. The invitation to live holy lives does not leave us bereft of the support needed in working out this call to holiness. God has given us a gift to assist us in this process of becoming holy—the gift of Jesus Christ. Jesus is a path for us. He does not just hand us a blueprint for holiness; he walks the way with us. Over the years one of the consoling voices of Jesus has been the echo of his words, *"Abide in me as I abide in you"* (John 15:4, NRSV). There is no finer description of holiness than in the mutual abiding expressed in those few words.

Paul strongly implies that we are made holy because of our obedience to the truth and he warmly encourages us to love one another intensely from a pure heart. Our renewal takes place because we have chosen to accept the invitation to be faithful to what lasts forever: the abiding Word of God. Although the fragility of our lives and the flowers of the fields wither away, God's Word endures. Could it be that because each of us is a Word of God, we too, in some mysterious and miraculous way, will be counted in with what endures forever? The very thought is enough to provide us with a lifetime of meditation.

Remember, then, that we are holy and we have been asked to love one another intensely. Let us bend our ears in obedient listening to this call to live forever in the abiding Word of God.

Reflection and Prayer

- Go to the prose poem "The Beautiful Struggle" on page 124. Read it through thoughtfully, placing your focus on the third stanza. These words emphasize the truth that we are called to become holy, right in the midst of the hubbub of daily life. We don't have to go to heaven to become holy. It begins right here. Meditate on this.

- Paul speaks of us being born anew through the abiding Word of God. What is your understanding of God's Word being abiding? How can you be part of that abiding Word?

- What is your understanding of holiness? Reflect on people you know whose lives you consider to be holy.

O Abiding Word of God,

I am bending my ear toward your invitation to be holy. I am bending my ear to deep listening. Teach me to be obedient to your belief so that I too might live forever—forever caught up in your abiding Word. Make me holy, O God, and let it be a holiness that is not flashy. I will be happy with a quiet godliness that enables others to feel comfortable in my presence. To love intensely is my fondest wish. Teach me to abide so that I may be a word of healing for a long, long time. **Oh, may it come to pass!**

7. What's Enough?

Prayerfully read Luke 12:22-34.

I tell you, do not worry. (v. 22)

As I sit in my friend's tree house *romancing the word*, I am blessed to be surrounded by the voices of creation. Leaves rustle. Birds sing! Grass grows! The wind blows! Flowers bloom! On the ground below the birds scratch for food, breaking up the earth to harvest worms. The birds also feast from the feeders that hang on tree branches. As they eat their midday meal I read the words of Jesus to them. *"Notice the ravens: they do not sow or reap; they have neither storehouse nor barn, yet God feeds them"* (v. 24).

Jesus' words are good medicine for all of us who are called to trust in Providence. How insightful are we at recognizing God's providential care in good times and in hard times? Equanimity is a quality worthy of our reflection. Equanimity is simply opening our hearts to what is—letting go of all judgments about fairness. It is accepting the challenge to be grateful for what we have even if it doesn't measure up to what our colleagues have.

We struggle with the temptation to hoard and stockpile, to build bigger houses, to create exclusive neighborhoods. Hoarding ordinarily comes from insecurity. Our affluent society appears to be imprisoned by a paralyzing fear that there won't be enough. Actually, the *enough* question haunts us all. Do I have enough? Do I have enough food, enough stylish clothes, enough status and power, enough influential friends, enough gadgets that will make my life easier, enough possessions to be accepted by my popular peers? It is easy to become obsessed with accumulating things that add nothing to my heart's dearest desire.

Do I ever consider that some people really don't have enough? While I fret over designer clothes to go to a party, there are those who wonder how they will buy shoes for their children. These people understandably might raise an eyebrow over a gospel that suggests they shouldn't worry about what to eat or wear. Yet the irony of it is, these are often the people who practice equanimity best.

How different our lives might be if we could learn to put the emphasis on storing up the kind of gifts that neither rust nor fade. What if we were to ask another kind of question? Do I have enough compassion to notice the person who needs my assistance? Do I have enough gratitude to appreciate the gifts I've been given? Do I have enough integrity not to hoard more than I need? Do I have enough joy to create a comfortable home in the house where I live? Do I have enough trust to believe I will be amply cared for? Do I have enough hospitality to share what I have with others? Do I have enough wisdom to recognize the things that truly make me happy? Do I have enough contentment to keep me from obsessing over things beyond my means? Although we may not have arrived at the graced state of being totally free from desiring things beyond our reach, let us hope that we have not lost our ability to recognize that we are richly blessed even when we don't have everything we want.

Contentment is a treasure. Another treasure is our ability to enjoy the gifts we have without excessive craving for more. I once received a greeting card that asked a provocative question: "If you aren't happy with what you have, how could you be happier with more"? Take that question to your heart for reflection.

When people's lives become complicated and overburdened, they sometimes begin to discuss ways of living a more simple life. But what is a simple life? Surely it doesn't mean that we have to move to the country, raise cows and chickens, and grow all the vegetables we eat. Might it rather be a call to learn how to live more attentively? Could it be a nudge from our deep self to discern the things that truly lift our spirits and bring us joy?

"Consider the lilies, how they grow: they neither toil nor spin" (v. 27, NRSV). Jesus' words about the beauty of the lilies and the goodness of God's care for all creatures might be our wake-up call. Wake up and recognize the things that bring you peace. The poet Emily Dickinson once said that the only commandment she really took seriously was, "consider the lilies." Perhaps it is time for us to consider the lilies. The flowers of the fields will wither and fade but our memory of them can live forever.

When Jesus' words begin to sound naïve and foreign to the twenty-first century in which we live, let us try to look through the words, in between the words, and underneath the words to a deeper truth that lingers in the shadow of the Word.

Reflection and Prayer

- What's *enough* seems like an innocent and simple question. It is, however, a very big and difficult question. Spend some time with this question. What about you? What's enough? This is a question to pray with rather than answer.

- If you were going to simplify your life, what are some small ways you might want to begin?

O Beautiful Creator,

In your magnificent world of creation teach me to be content but never settled and uncaring. Reveal to me how to use things well and enjoy them without clinging and hoarding. I want to live with open hands. Give me a heart for sharing. Open my eyes to beauty so that I may always remember your command to "consider the lilies." Instill in me an awareness of the healing power of creation. Don't ever let me turn away from the hard questions. Let me live simply, beautifully, and generously all the days of my life. **May it come to pass!**

8. The Limp of Blessing

Prayerfully read Genesis 32:1-33.

> *You told me, O LORD, "Go back to the land of your birth,*
> *and I will be good to you." (v. 10)*

In preparation for your prayer with this text from the book of Genesis, read again the famous story of the stolen blessing (Gen 27). Whatever your feelings about that stolen blessing, begin this reflection in company with Jacob, who, in obedience to God, is returning to his homeland. The stolen blessing is weighing heavily on his mind; or is it fear of retaliation from Esau that is causing the weight? Most likely it is a mixture of fear, regret, and love. Jacob wants to be received with love and forgiveness by Esau and so he does what any of us might do in a similar circumstance. He sends gifts ahead of him, hoping that the material gifts might assuage any leftover anger Esau might be harboring against him.

This action also hints at Jacob's realization of his need for forgiveness. The gifts have been sent ahead, but the season of forgiveness and reconciliation has not yet been celebrated. The word *give* is part of *forgive.* This seems to imply that forgiveness is a gift. It requires both giving and receiving.

In this beautifully human story we are given a glimpse of Jacob's cleverness and resourcefulness, his vulnerability and love for his people. He divides his people up into two camps, with hope that, just in case Esau comes to him with animosity and revenge rather than compassion and forgiveness, at least one of the camps might be spared.

Jacob then ponders how he once crossed the Jordan with nothing but his staff. Now he is returning with a vast company of kindred people, many herds, and many possessions. With a prayer on his lips, he sends the two companies ahead of him while he stays behind in the camp to wrestle with timeless questions.

Rising in the middle of the night, he takes his family, along with their possessions, safely across the ford of the Jabbok. Then once again, he is without company, possessing nothing but the raw material of himself. In that awful moment he is left alone to face a mysterious visitor who struggles with him until dawn.

Jacob's vigil through the night is profoundly moving. If I were to name this experience, I would call it "the season before forgiveness." We can only surmise the inner turmoil that surfaces during this long night of battle. In praying with Jacob's struggle, try to put yourself in his place. Spend some time reflecting on your own struggles with the angel of God. As you name those struggles, name also your adversaries.

I will not let you go until you bless me. (v. 27)

The divine being who wrestled with Jacob didn't seem to mind losing the battle. This was a significant spiritual struggle, through which Jacob had to pass. It was obvious that Jacob was powerful, relentless, and sincere in his battle with his own demons, and with the divine. Thus, the Holy One who struggled with him heard his appeal for a blessing: *"I will not let you go until you bless me,"* Jacob avows.

He was blessed with a new name and a limp. This limp of blessing was evidence that he had contended with God, and had won the battle. His new name suggested that the old Jacob who crossed the Jordan so many years ago no longer existed. A new person was born out of that divine struggle.

Do we not all carry within us the limp of blessing? The holy limp that proclaims both our vulnerability and our strength! And when we rise from our battles, do we sometimes discover that we too have been given new names?

Contemplate your holy limp and your new name! Rejoice in the spiritual warrior you are becoming. In the beautiful struggle of daily life you too limp along in glory. No matter how many battle scars you possess, you also possess an inner spiritual power. It is this power that will help you rise above the obstacles that stand between you and your faithful, steadfast heart!

Stepping back into our biblical story for a moment, note that Jacob was curious about his adversary. Who was this mysterious visitor; whose embrace was it that enabled Jacob to forgive himself? When he asked the stranger for a name, the name was withheld. Jacob's desire to know the name of the one with whom he struggled is certainly understandable. *"Tell me your name,"* Jacob pleads. One's name holds a certain power. We would like to be able to name our struggles so as to understand them. Like Jacob, we too find ourselves wondering, Who is this divine being by whom we are daily challenged? Who is this one who keeps wrestling us down, opening our hearts? We too must learn to live without complete answers. It is called faith; this holy wrestler has no name, except the name we give him or her in each of our spiritual struggles.

And so our friend Jacob limps away. He is limping toward forgiveness. Let us limp with him.

Reflection and Prayer

- In your personal life can you relate to Jacob's struggle with the mysterious visitor—the angel of God? Who is that visitor for you?

- You may not be used to thinking symbolically but our spiritual struggles or our religious experiences often give us new names. Meditate on one of your recent spiritual experiences and see if a new name might emerge for you.

- Is there anyone in your life that you need to forgive? If so, pray about this forgiveness. The power to forgive is already within you. It may only need to be awakened.

O Divine Wrestler,

When I come to you seeking transformation, I am often faced with a small battle. It is a struggle that I have named *beautiful* because out of this struggle blessings ordinarily emerge. For my prayer of struggle I have chosen Jacob's mantra, *"I will not let you go until you bless me"*! Enable me to stay in the struggle until the blessing arrives. I will allow myself to be vulnerable. That very vulnerability is my limp, but it is also my blessing. O Transforming One, you have wounded me, yet you have not disappointed me. I am grateful for the blessing of all my new names. **Thank you for your presence in the beautiful struggle of daily life.**

Poetic Summary of Chapter Three

The Beautiful Struggle

Much of the beauty of daily life is invisible while it is happening. Many moons later we look back and see cobwebbed strands of beauty poking their faces out of buried memories—memories that bring both tears and laughter, sorrow and joy. Through windows of the past we are given visions of the incredible faith, hope, and love lived out in the midst of the beautiful struggle of daily life.

We see visions of our parents laboring through headaches and heartaches we never noticed before; too little money in the bank and too few communication skills to know how to say *I love you*, yet loving us all the same, in the midst of the beautiful struggle of daily life.

We strive to bear witness to this grace-filled struggle, living with sacramental attitudes around the altar of daily life. With our steadfast love we sanctify the simple materials of each day. We are priestly people, bruised, burdened, and ennobled from each day's work. The work is our love made visible in the midst of the beautiful struggle of daily living.

God becomes flesh again each day. Christ shines forth from the temple of our beings. We build and we create with the tools we have been given: our expressive hands and eager feet, our deep-scanning eyes and listening ears, our adventuresome spirits, our inquisitive minds and yearning hearts. Let us never belittle the gifts we've been given to lift beauty out of the struggle.

We build the reign of God right here in the midst of this daily struggle. We do not have to wait until we die to go to heaven. Let's go to heaven right now. Let us build heaven on earth by believing in our own goodness—we who have been created in the image of God. Let us feed on the truth that the image of God in us is to be our hope here in the midst of the beautiful struggle of daily life.

Chapter Four

Don't
Look Back

I have always been sweetly haunted by the gospel command that suggests we are not ready to live in the kingdom of God if we put our hand to the plough and keep looking back (Luke 9:62). The looking back is distraction. The looking back is a lack of commitment. The looking back is an inability to trust. The looking back suggests a lack of interest, a divided heart, or at least an unfocused heart.

The plough suggests purpose, intention, a goal or plan for the ground of our lives. Each of us is sacred ground waiting for a plough to open up the soil so that the Word of God may have a welcoming space to grow. The plough attempts to move away the obstacles that prevent the Word from entering into the ground of our being and taking root in us.

Excessive looking back prevents us from seeing where we are, and where we are going. Living in the past is not helpful. If we are always looking back with regret, or perhaps contemplating that we've made a mistake, it is difficult to be committed to the task at hand. Naturally, there will be times when we must discern whether the work we are doing is too small for our souls. Some changes may be necessary. Perhaps we may need to be doing something else.

In this chapter, *don't look back*; you are to reflect on commitment. The Scripture texts, offered for your prayer, will invite you to root yourself in the Word of God. Put your whole self onto the spiritual path. Listen deeply to God's plan for you. Be faithful to your goal and your dreams. Trust! Be committed! Be rooted!

If you want to grow in holiness, you must learn to sink your roots deeply into many good things.

1. Don't Look Back

Prayerfully read Luke 9:51-62.

> *No one who sets a hand to the plow*
> *and looks to what was left behind*
> *is fit for the kingdom of God. (v. 62)*

In praying this passage from the Gospel of Luke we are given an opportunity to reflect on and keep company with some of Jesus' disciples as well as some of his would-be followers. For Jesus to go to Jerusalem through Samaria was an invitation to trouble. An age-old quarrel between Jews and Samaritans suggests that Samaria might not be an attractive stopping place. Why would Jesus even look for hospitality in Samaria unless perhaps he was attempting to soften that old quarrel by offering hospitality? There are times when asking for hospitality becomes a way of offering hospitality. It didn't work, though, and the disciples' reaction to rejection is interesting. They wanted to call down a fire of destruction upon those who refused to welcome them. The kind of fire that Jesus would want to call down upon those who rejected him would probably be a very different kind of fire from what the disciples were ready to offer. Jesus' fire would most likely be the fire of love, compassion, and forgiveness.

As Jesus continues his journey to Jerusalem he meets others along the way whose hearts have been touched by his message. They too express a desire to become disciples. To each of these he offers a challenge. Try to find yourself in each person who desires to follow Jesus. Let Jesus' answer to them become the core of your prayer.

To the first person who requests to follow him, Jesus explains that he has nowhere to lay his head. To put it bluntly, are you willing to follow a homeless person? What wisdom would you expect to find in the life of someone who has nothing? You may want to feed and assist one who is homeless. But follow them? Set up tent with them? Gather from the storehouse of their wisdom—or even believe they have any wisdom to offer? Jesus was aware that it would be difficult for anyone to truly cast their lots with him; thus he cautions this would-be follower with the reminder that he has no home to call his own.

The second challenge sounds even harsher. For Jewish people, caring for the aged was a great honor and a grave responsibility. Does it seem like an unreasonable request to take care of responsibilities at home before trailing off after some itinerant preacher? We don't know that the father of the one who wanted to follow Jesus had actually died. It may very well be that this was a request to stay at home until all responsibilities had been taken care of, including that of attending the needs of elderly parents through their final hours. Jesus' seemingly harsh answer may be a way of saying, *you must learn to let go of your obsessive need to have everything in order before attending the deepest desires of your heart.* Who among us cannot relate to such advice? How good are we in being obedient to our heart's greatest longing? Or, have we even considered what the deepest yearning of our heart is?

Finally, we have Jesus' challenge to the one who merely wanted to say goodbye to friends and family. Jesus' answer to this person has inspired me since my youth. *"No one who sets a hand to the plow and looks to what was left behind is fit for the kingdom of God"* (v. 62). I'm not sure why this text made such an impression on me as an adolescent. Perhaps it was because the plow was a very real part of my childhood. I remember plowing the field with my father and I knew the importance of keeping an eye on the ground being plowed. Or, it may stem from the reality that I sometimes struggle with a temptation to look back on lost moments of my life with regret. I have always been tremendously challenged by people who are prophetic—those who, when hearing the call, gathered up the moments of God's visitation and surrendered their lives to generosity, devotion, and commitment. Prophets from biblical times and prophets of today stir my heart to greater awareness. I am grateful for these role models who awaken me to truths I can't quite reach on my own. They call me to authenticity. There is no gift I would rather have than that of being authentic.

> *Do not look back. And do not dream about the future, either.*
> *It will neither give you back the past, nor satisfy*
> *your other daydreams.*
> *Your duty, your reward—your destiny—are here and now.*
> *(Dag Hammarskjold)*

Although I would like to live each moment with authenticity, I fail miserably. I realize that the present moment is a pearl of great price—a jewel given to me freely. Yet I have not learned the art of joyfully receiving the bold invitation of the moments with an awareness of the enriching possibilities within my reach. I would like to be more authentically present to the moments of each day. Yet looking back to lost moments hinders rather than helps. There's an old bushman adage that counsels, *"Don't look back"*; this is sage advice. If I am always looking back with regret, my heart is in two places. A heart in two places is a heart in no place. Certainly there will be indecisive moments in our lives yet if this hesitancy persists as a life pattern, it suggests a fear of commitment. My reluctance to commit needs acknowledgment and prayer because underneath my overly cautious heart lives that original longing to risk.

Have you ever made a commitment that required a whole-hearted *yes*? Can you recall a moment in your lifetime when you gave your heart to some cause and didn't count the cost? Do you remember an experience in your life in which you determinedly said *no* to halfhearted living? If you could paint a picture of a deeply committed person, what would it look like? What colors would you use? What sounds would be in the picture? What words would you choose to write about such a person?

Have you been tempted to look back in regret on a moment when you once joyfully surrendered your all? Have you ever found yourself taking back little pieces of a self you thought you had generously surrendered to God?

To give oneself to something or someone for a lifetime is a torturous thought for many people these days. Commitment is a colossal struggle in this new age in which we live. Take time today to evaluate and celebrate the healthy commitments in your life.

Reflection and Prayer

- A human person on fire with love for the way of Christ and setting that fire ablaze with action and contemplation is one of my images of commitment. Do you have a favorite description of commitment? Write a little paragraph of your own insight about just what it means to live a life of commitment.

- Do you recall moments in your life when you have wavered between wholeheartedness and halfheartedness?

Jesus,

Your invitation has not been forgotten. There was no RSVP so I have dilly-dallied in my response. I want to be your disciple but I struggle with the cost. All? The cost is all? There are moments when I find such extravagance attractive. My whole-heart leaps for joy at the very thought of this prodigal gift of self. But my half-heart cringes at the thought of having nothing left for it. Perhaps if I could get my half-heart to make friends with my whole-heart, the result would be a harmonious friendship that would bless my burning desire to be your disciple. But my half-heart is so cautious and not too keen about the exquisite risk of giving all. **O Unfailing Love, please be patient while I work this out.**

2. The Practice of Being Ready

Prayerfully read 1 Peter 4:7-11.

The end of all things is at hand. (v. 7)

You probably remember that as we drew near to the year 2000, the millennium, there was much talk about the end of the world. In Scripture, references to the *end times* often include descriptive language that may create an aura of fear. This is frequently accompanied by warnings about the dangers of being caught unprepared. In this sermon from the First Letter of Peter there is a very pastoral tone filled with encouraging suggestions about how we should live so as to be always ready to meet God.

These words from Peter can serve as a lovely preparation for death. They are an excellent means to appraise the quality of our lives. Rather than fill our minds with fearful images of the end times, why not prayerfully reflect about the end of our lives on this earth? Read again this text from the First Letter of Peter, looking at it as a way to live before you die. These few words could serve as a lifelong preparation for death. We do not know when the end of the world will be nor do we know the day of our death. We do know, however, that we will die. Death is as natural as birth. If we can allow each moment to be a sacrament of dying, then we will go through the door of death alive. Let us also try to fill our hearts with gratitude for the presence and workings of Jesus in our lives and in the lives of our biblical ancestors.

We experience a variety of end times throughout our lives: the end of jobs, the end of relationships, loss of health, fading youth, the end of each day, the end of life on earth. Our children leave home. We retire. Our faith begins to waver. How are we to prepare for these end times? We are to be watchful, attentive, disciplined, and calm so that we may be able to pray.

> *Therefore, be serious and sober for prayers. (v. 7)*

Praying when we are anxious and fearful is difficult. A classic work titled *Letters of the Scattered Brotherhood* encourages us during the turbulent times to sink down three fathoms beneath the storm where the quiet is. During the stormy times, of course, most of us don't have a clue as to how to get below the storm. Have you ever tried to pray when you are in a total stew? It is not easy. It takes practice to remain calm. However, it will greatly enrich our prayer life if we make the effort to let this advice become a reality in our lives. There is a place way down below the anxiety, underneath the storm, where the peace of Christ waits for us.

> *Above all, let your love for one another be intense,*
> *because love covers a multitude of sins. (v. 8)*

These words suggest that if we place more emphasis on our responsibility to love, praying during the troubled times might become more attractive. It is easy to go about our day doing good works out of obligation while forgetting that it is our love that makes the work good. If we are not attentive to love, our good works can slip into the realm of duty. Our tasks become projects, and the ones we are serving become objects.

> *Be hospitable to one another without complaining. (v. 9)*

As part of this week's prayer—practice, take time to contemplate the ones you are serving. Contemplate love. How well do you love? How do you keep your love constant? How long has it been since you've spent time *being with* instead of *doing for*? It is in the *being* aspect of your life that you practice hospitality. You are to be hospitable to others, Peter says, without complaining. That means that you may sometimes be called to be hospitable to someone you judge unworthy of your hospitality. Let Christ be the judge of that person's worthiness. You are simply called to be a welcoming presence. Saint Benedict picks up this thought and uses it in his Rule for monastic communities. "Above all else we admonish them to refrain from grumbling" (RB 40.9). We who live in any kind of household can benefit from that wise counsel. We are to be a welcoming presence for one another without complaining. After all, if we murmur, can our service to one another even be called hospitality?

Whoever preaches, let it be with the words of God;
whoever serves, let it be with the strength that God supplies . . .
(v. 11)

What excellent advice this is! I have often prayed that I could preach without sounding preachy. The word *preach* has never been appealing to me. Still, I know many people whose preaching sounds more like teaching; this I can relate to because I live in constant awareness of my need to be guided. In the gospels we are often told that people believed in Jesus because he preached with authority. Most likely, he preached with authority because he spent time with the One who was the Source of his authority—the One he called Abba Father. This Source of life is available to each of us. If you want to preach, teach, and serve as Jesus and his disciples modeled for us, pray for a heart open to being taught by God. The best teachers of the Word of God are the ones who take time to abide in the Word.

The same can be said about serving others. This Scripture text clearly states that our service to others is possible because of the strength that is provided to us by God. We discover our strength through embracing the Word. In living our lives around the Word of God we are given strength for all the end times through which we must journey.

> . . . *so that in all things God may be glorified. (v. 11)*

Everything we do, no matter how small, can highlight the presence of God in our lives. It is to God we give the glory for our teaching, our loving, and our serving! If we practice listening to the moments, the light of God's presence will shine through all of our actions.

Reflection and Prayer

- In stormy, turbulent moments practice conscious breathing. This empowers you to stay calm so you are able to pray with greater attention. The peace of Christ waits for you in the eye of the storm. What is your experience of trying to remain calm in the midst of chaos? Have you discovered anything that works for you?

- Do you believe in your power to love intensely even when it isn't easy? Try contemplating this kind of love.

- Embrace the Word of God each day. This will help you remember the source of strength for serving others.

O Source of Vibrant Life,

Prepare my heart to live luminously in any kind of weather. In dark and stormy times show me the way to remain calm so that I may find the love in me that is always saying its prayers. Bring into my vision the strength I thought was lost. And just when I think I have no word of comfort to offer, reveal to me the words you have already given me. May I live in such a way that I am always ready to die and always ready to live. May I live in such a way that in all things you may be glorified! **Amen.**

3. If Only You Had Listened

Prayerfully read Isaiah 48:12-21.

> *Yes, my hand laid the foundations of the earth;*
> *my right hand spread out the heavens.*
> *When I call them, they stand forth at once. (v. 13)*

These words offer us an awesome image of the obedience of creation. When creation is summoned, it comes into being. It listens to the voice of the Creator and steps forth singing the song of life. We too are part of God's creation. Are we as faithful to God's voice calling us into being as is creation? We begin this meditation pondering the faithfulness of creation. Creation waits for the voice of God. Creation listens. Underline the word *listen*. We too are led by God. We are taught by God. Yet, often we fail to listen with the inner obedience seen in creation. In the New Jerusalem translation of this same text we read the words, "My hand laid the foundations of earth and my right hand spread out the heavens. I summon them and they all present themselves together" (v. 13, NJB). These words are a magnificent portrayal of creation's obedience to the Creator. Creation listens! Creation stands forth when called!

> *Listening looks easy, but it's not simple.*
> *Every head is a world. (Cuban Proverb)*

Does this Cuban proverb hold out a clue to our difficulty in listening? Is it the head that gives us problems? Creation doesn't have a head to worry about. It simply responds to an inner natural call to grow, to be beautiful, and to obey the elements of earth.

Everything seems to flow forth in harmony—all from a Divine Source. The created cosmos appears to possess an inner obedience that we poor mortals often lack. I wonder! Do we really lack this inner depth of response or have we not fully discovered it?

> *If only you had listened to my commandments!*
> *Your prosperity would have been like a river*
> *and your saving justice like the waves of the sea.*
> *(v. 18, NJB)*

As I leaned toward the words of this Scripture text, the echo of "if only" lingered in my soul. If only you had listened, if only you had been alert! These words struck a chord in my heart. They imprinted themselves in my being. If only you had listened . . . My years of pondering the Scriptures through *lectio divina* have taught me to be patient with words that linger.

Listen to words that refuse to go away. When this happens, bring forth your listening ear. Try to discern why these particular words have taken hold of you. How is this text meant to be your teacher? What truth do you need to hear again in your life? Hearken! Listen! Pay attention! If only you had been attentive! In contemplating the Word of God, specific texts may come as a personal summons to listen to the One who called you into being, the Creator who in unseen ways is still fashioning you. Like Israel, perhaps you are being called to listen more attentively?

In this text from Isaiah, we can observe the hardening of the heart of Israel. We note the people's refusal to listen. This theme can certainly be extended to our own hearts in this new era. Yahweh is shown as our teacher and guide, leading us on the good path. The supposition here is that because we have not been alert to divine guidance and have not listened to the voice of God, our joy is not as deep as it might have been. Our integrity and faithfulness are not as complete as God intended them to be. Each of us is in a little exile—harboring feelings of abandonment. It is often in moments of discouragement that the echo of God's voice breaks in: If only you had listened . . .

In praying with this text, the part of us that feels exiled may begin to lament: "Oh, if only I had listened to the grace within and around me, my life would be richer, happier, and more wholesome." Although this may be true, it is never healthy to dwell in a house of "if only."

Rather than remaining stuck in the sorrows that have come from not listening, let's choose to draw strength from those who have listened well. Listening is an art. We can pattern our lives after the artist-saints from our ranks who have learned the art of listening. We too can learn to listen. In this closing litany, let your prayerful response be, *Teach me the art of listening.*

Isaiah, age-old prophet of hope—you turned your ear toward a voice that asked you to speak for God . . .

Mary of Nazareth—you listened to an angel inviting you to say yes to what you could not yet understand . . .

Joseph, foster father of Jesus—you listened to a dream that changed history . . .

Jesus, you withdrew to the desert hills—absorbed in God, you listened . . .

Mary Magdalene—you listened to an intense love that set up its tent in your heart . . .

Dorothy Day—you too listened to a love that heard the cries of the poor . . .

*Martin Luther King Jr.—you listened to the beauty and integrity
of a people, crying out in their exile . . .
Oscar Romero and all Central American martyrs—thank you
for listening to the powerless and dispossessed . . .*

These and so many more have been alert to the voice of God throughout the ages. Add your own prophetic saints to this list of listeners. You will find them waiting in the archives of your heart. They bent their ears in obedience to the voice of God saying, "I am sending you!" May we learn from them the art of listening! May we learn from them the art of putting one's hand to the plow and not looking back! May we learn from them the beauty and pain of commitment!

In reflecting on the art of listening, perhaps we will discover that we have listened better than we thought. Focusing on our negligence is seldom helpful. Let us focus, instead, on our desire to learn how to be obedient to God's Word.

As a Native American proverb reminds us, *"Listen, or your tongue will keep you deaf!"*

Reflection and Prayer

- How well do you listen?

- Can you perceive that, like creation, you have an inner ability to listen? How good are you in bending your ear in obedience to the voice of God?

- How do you experience listening to God in daily life?

- Are you aware of this kind of listening when it is happening, or are you more likely to reflect on it afterwards?

- How might your life be different if you lived *truly alert*?

O Ancient Listener,

I hear your supportive voice whispering to me, "don't look back to the times you didn't say your prayers or to the times you turned away from someone who needed your love. Look, instead, all around you, within you, above you, below you. There is always something new unfolding. It is never too late to listen." Your voice is dear and I acknowledge the truth of it. Yes, you are still calling my name. New melodies arise each day. I now lean toward the small experiences of each moment with eagerness. I put away regrets as I step into a new hour of listening. **O Ancient Listener, teach me the art of listening!**

4. Away with Your Troubled Hearts

Prayerfully read John 14:1-14.

Do not let your hearts be troubled!
You have faith in God; have faith also in me. (v. 1)

To live with untroubled hearts in these times is a tall order. Actually these words of Jesus are deeper than an order. They are an invitation—a summons to trust. Is it possible, in a world such as ours, to live without anxiety? To put away our anxiety, of course, does not mean to cast away our care. Rather, with the absence of anxiety we stand a greater chance of discerning ways to direct the care that is in our hearts. We become more aware of our potential to love and God's desire for us to live in trust with one another.

The Scriptures are full to the brim with invitations to trust. *"Though war be waged against me, even then do I trust"* (Ps 27:3). This is only one of the psalmist's countless proclamations of trust. We are asked to put our faith in Jesus instead of moving through our days with troubled hearts. But how does one do that on the difficult days? Amid the mounting rubble of war torn countries, in the presence of so many homeless people and abused children, in the midst of all the violence that sweeps through our world, in the animosity and distrust that keeps growing between political parties—does it even make sense to trust? Well, of course, it does make sense to trust. Adding our suspicion and despair to a world that is already fearful is certainly not helpful for the healing of the world. In the midst of all that is horrible in this world there is a God who still has confidence in us. Believing the truth of that statement can help to restore our trust and faith. Do we trust the good in our own lives?

In our meditation for today Jesus is actually preparing his disciples for his departure from them. He tells them that if they have faith in him, they will do even greater works than he has done. This is his promise also for his present-day disciples. It is his promise to stay with us always and to continue his work through us and in us. To accomplish this, we are asked to pray in his name. One way of praying in the name of Jesus is to totally immerse ourselves in the risen Christ so that just as Jesus told Philip, *"Whoever has seen me has seen the Father"* (v. 9), we too can say, "Whoever sees me sees Christ." Whoever sees Macrina sees Christ! Whoever sees (add your name) sees Christ.

Jesus' intimate relationship with the one he calls his Father simply sings of trust. At key points in his ministry, times when he faced loss, needed to make decisions, or suffered from the weariness of the day's work, Jesus went away to be in communion with the Father. This "going away" suggests a conscious choice to seek restoration and to rely upon the One who sent him.

And now he is going away again. This time, though, his going away has an air of mystery about it. His followers suspect that something they don't understand is about to happen. They want answers. *"Master,"* Thomas pleads, *"we do not know where you are going; how can we know the way?"* (v. 5). Thomas's anxiety raises a question in my own searching soul: where are you going? It's a good question. I could take a walk with that question every morning. Loved ones are dying all around me—too young and too often. I wonder what their response might have been had I asked them, *where are you going?*

It's a good question to ask not only on our deathbed but also every day. *Just where are we going?* And what about this place Jesus promises to prepare for us? Can we have a taste of *this place* while on earth? I think we can. Jesus tried to teach us how to make the desires of God's heart our own heart's longing. Like Jesus, we too find ourselves *going away* for days of quiet to prepare a place for the will of God in our lives. Thus always, wherever we go we carry within us *the longing of God. God's* dreams for the world reside in our hearts.

Sometimes we get lost and have to search out *the way*. Those of us who depend on maps can appreciate the apostles' lament about not knowing *the way*. Give me the directions. How do I get to this place? These words conjure up memories of hiking in the desert near Tucson. Time and time again I was told, "don't forget to build your cairn." A cairn is a marker, usually a pile of stones to help you stay on track.

Perhaps Jesus is our cairn. *"I am the way and the truth and the life,"* he claims (v. 6). We will find *the way* to communion with God by watching Jesus. Where is the road that leads to life? The way to the place of life is the way of love and compassion. It is the way of justice and forgiveness. It is the path of generosity and joy. Sometimes it is the road of suffering. It is also the path of hope and trust. Jesus is our cairn on the way to the Great Abiding. We learn to walk this path full of concern for others. We carry within us the *dream of God*. What must be done in our world can be done through us. Whoever sees us sees Christ.

O may it come to pass that we can live with untroubled hearts, free of anxiety yet with hearts full of care.

Reflection and Prayer

A troubled, anxious heart is like a little person. It has its own personality and we do need to learn how to be with it. Here are some ways of being present to your troubled heart.

- Take it for a walk in the early morning hours when few people are around.
- Sit with it for long hours gazing into the waters of the lake.
- Take it to a window at night. Turn out the light; open the curtain and gaze at the stars.
- Light a candle. Sit down and empty your dear head of thoughts to the extent possible. Become one with your breathing. Let your breath become your prayer.
- Write a poem for it! Sing it a song!
- Take it for dancing lessons!
- Listen to a beautiful piece of music with it.
- Introduce it to the wide-open spaces of a meadow and fresh air.
- Have tea with it and maybe even invite a friend.
- Take it to church for holy hour.

Was time spent with your troubled heart magical, mystical, miraculous, or medicinal? If this was a multiple-choice test, I would have to check all of the above. We have such good medicine right at our fingertips. It is a mystery why we don't use it regularly.

O Heart of My Heart,

Where did you go when you went away? Did you move deeper into my heart? I have discovered that you left cures for my troubled heart all around me. I am trying to make use of them: fresh air, deep breaths, stars and wide-open spaces, music and song, light and darkness, poetry, prayer, beauty, and more. What good medicine for my soul! It is always in my reach and for this I thank you. Keep moving deeper into my heart. Teach me the dance of trust. **O Heart of my Heart, dance me into the lives of all who need healing.**

5. This Tremendous Love

Prayerfully read Matthew 5:38-48.

> *You have heard that it was said,*
> *"An eye for an eye and a tooth for a tooth."*
> *But I say to you, offer no resistance to one who is evil. (vv. 38-39)*

In January of 2001, just after the Jubilee Year, we executed eleven people in the United States. It was a gloomy beginning of the twenty-first century, a disheartening wake of the new millennium. I read through the descriptions of the horrendous acts of cruelty those *guilty ones* committed and something akin to rage rose up in my heart. It is easy for me to understand that many people would still hold on to the Old Testament adage, "an eye for an eye and a tooth for a tooth." In the face of such atrocities, how can Jesus' words, "offer no resistance . . ." hold any credibility?

There is something unnerving about Jesus' teaching that we offer no resistance to injury. It sounds like an impossible ideal even for those of us who would like to take his message to our hearts for genuine consideration. We may be tempted to remind Jesus that he is not preaching only to saints; the rest of us are trying to listen also. On the other hand, the very fact that Jesus is teaching in this manner suggests that he sees quality material in us—the stuff of which saints are made.

A lot of space in the world is still filled with hate. As followers of Jesus we have no option except to try to fill up these spaces with love. What might happen if, instead of holding on to our desire for revenge, we would endeavor to fill up all places of hate with love? Where hate reigns, love can reign! Where love reigns, there is no room for hate!

Perhaps we should change the way we pray. So often we ask for what we want rather than what we need. Why not pray for compassion for those who have hurt us? Compassion is good medicine. If we allow love and compassion to replace hate and indifference, a new morality will arise within us. This new morality will reflect the teachings of Jesus.

The most difficult part of the call to love, for many of us, is to love those who do not seem worthy of our love. Yet surely this is what we are asked to do when Jesus tells us to love our enemies. Love is a spiritual practice. It doesn't happen automatically. We have to practice loving. Take a moment to underline the word *practice.* It means exactly that! We practice! If we want to excel in something like dancing, ice skating, music, gymnastics, or any kind of sport, it doesn't surprise us to be told we must practice. What about opening our hearts to those who have wounded us? What about forgiving? What about loving our enemies? What about becoming who we really are? Might we need some practice?

Being and becoming take time, and commitment to stay open is at the very core of what it means to be a person. (Mark Nepo)[1]

Practice opening your heart! If you go deep enough into the chambers of your heart, you will discover a place of love waiting for you. It is a place where *getting even* doesn't matter. I recall overhearing two kids talking about forgiving and getting even so long ago I can't remember the details. But this I do remember: the discussion concerned whether we had to forgive and what it meant to get even. One of the children suggested that getting even meant standing in the same place. I seriously doubt that she had any idea how profound her answer was. If you think about this for a moment, the truth of the answer may catch up with you. Isn't that exactly what we do when we try to get even with someone? We put ourselves in the same place where he or she is. The problem of when we need to forgive was taken care of with a quick dismissal. The other child with a matter-of-fact flair said, "Oh I don't have to forgive; I'm not a Catholic." Forgiveness, of course, crosses the bounds of all religions. There are no border-lines. Even if Jesus hadn't asked us to forgive, I believe there is a place in our hearts where we know that the path of forgiveness is the noble path. Perhaps the challenge is to not look back to all those reasons why we shouldn't forgive.

Jesus' invitation to love is a call to trust the seed of our own goodness—that saint-like quality that has been planted deep in our beings. There in that sacred place, we begin to understand that hatred only holds us in bondage, while forgiveness and love set us free. If we make every effort to trust that the love of Christ really is flowing through us and out of us into the lives of others, we will begin to experience the blessing of a newfound freedom. A deep peace settles over us. We too are loved in the midst of our sinfulness and inadequacies.

This loving place really does exist in us. It is from this place of freedom and peace that with practice in opening our hearts, we can turn the other cheek, walk the extra mile, or hand over our cloak to the one who wants to borrow.

In his book *Cherish Christ Above All*, Demetrius Dumm[2] emphasizes that the love we are to have for others is not merely human love that has somehow been blessed by God. He insists that it is the Divine Love transforming our human loving, so that our love is able to do what it could never do on its own. Moreover, he suggests that Jesus' mandate for us to love is not just a call to imitate the loving of Jesus. It is more like allowing the love of Jesus to flow through us for the good of others. His thoughts on this tremendous love flowing through us happily brings to memory a beautiful song by Briege O'Hare, titled "How Wonderful Is My Soul." The sentiments of the song echo Demetrius's thoughts. Nothing will ever bring us the peace we long for except God's love flowing through our being.

We will never grasp the wonder of our souls and our vast capacity for love until we learn to open our hearts to the people we are becoming. It is as though we are waiting for ourselves to arrive. We are watching ourselves emerge from the womb of our becoming. We are opening our lives to the love that is flowing through our being. Somewhere in the midst of this flowing we discover that just as we cannot become holy on our own, we cannot love all alone. My flowing flows into your flowing. Together we are a vessel of this tremendous love.

Reflection and Prayer

- You are a vessel of God's tremendous love! How do those words feel in your soul? In a practical way, what does it mean for you to be a vessel of love? Sit and pray with the beauty of this truth.

- Do you remember trying to fill a space of dissension or violence with love? Try to imagine a place in your life right now where you might get a little practice in doing just that.

- What are your thoughts on the morality of capital punishment? Have they changed over the years?

- Who have been some of the great models of love for you throughout your life? List some of these in your journal along with your reasons for choosing them.

O Love Tremendous and All-Embracing,

Draw me into the circle of your love. Do not permit me to love with only half a heart. Rather, let my love be a radical self-gift, an outpouring of my best self for the good of others. Tattoo your name on my heart. Have compassion on my feeble attempts to love, my reticence to give freely of my gifts and time. Grant that I may always remember it is your love flowing through my being, which makes it possible for me to love others. Do not allow me to squander your love. **Draw me into the circle of your love!**

6. A Rule of Life

Prayerfully read Philippians 4:4-9.

We are all beggars.
We are all members of a species that is not sufficient unto itself.
We are all creatures plagued
by unending doubts and restless, unsatisfied hearts.
(Johannes Baptist Metz)[3]

The restless, unsatisfied hearts of many people are leading them to seek a *rule of life* that can serve as a guide for their spiritual quest. Although these modern-day seekers do not necessarily want to live in a religious community or a monastery, they have a strong desire for a daily practice that will assist them in living their everyday lives with greater faithfulness to that part of life we name spiritual. Perhaps you are one of these seekers.

Sometimes when I am praying the Scriptures, a jewel rises up out of the pages that seems to sparkle more than all the other words of God. For me, Philippians 4:4-9 is one such jewel. If you are looking for a guide, this could serve as your *rule of life.*

From these holy words, I have gleaned a few necessary qualities that could be life companions for any of us. These qualities are joy, kindness, trust, gratitude, and peace. When embraced, any of these virtues can greatly enhance the quality of life in our households of faith.

In this reflection, I am going to walk through these virtues with you. Each virtue holds a unique grace for you. Watch for your special grace.

Rejoice in the Lord always. I shall say it again: rejoice! (v. 4)

What is joy and how does joy make its way into our lives? We are told to rejoice in the Lord but what if we can't find the joy for rejoicing? Two writers who have given me a wonderful insight into joy are Dom Marmion, a Benedictine abbot and spiritual teacher of the early twentieth century, and novelist Eugenia Price. Marmion suggests that "joy is the echo of God's life in us," while Eugenia Price says that "joy is God in the marrow of our bones." Joy: the echo of God's life! Joy: God in the marrow of our bones! These descriptions of joy are profoundly intimate. It is God who is the source and cause of our joy. This is the reason it is possible for a seed of joy to live, even in the heart of sorrow. The challenge we face, of course, is to learn how to tap into the joy that is a constant, though not always felt, presence in our lives. Spend some quality time with joy this week. Even in the midst of the anxieties and struggles that beset you each day, get in touch with the joy that abides in those hidden places of your soul. Accept it as one of your guides, an important part of your rule of life.

Your kindness should be known to all. (v. 5)

If you want to learn kindness, you must let go of your preoccupation with self. Kindness can be such a comfort to others. Your small gestures of kindness can be ways of being present to another: picking up an item someone dropped, holding open the door, listening intently to a story being told, offering a warm smile, writing a brief message rather than just signing your name to a birthday card. Faithfulness in the practice of little daily kindnesses can prepare us for that time when larger and more time-consuming opportunities present themselves. Living lives attuned to the daily needs of others is a form of kindness that can lead us to the even deeper kindness of compassion. Paul expresses this so well in his words, *"whatever is true, whatever is honorable, whatever is just, whatever is pure, whatever is lovely, whatever is gracious . . . think about these things"* (v. 8).

Have no anxiety at all . . . (v. 6)

Putting away anxiety requires trust. When Paul asks us to put away our anxieties and turn to God for all our needs, he is asking us to live in trust. Looking to God for our needs evokes the image of a child depending totally on beloved parents.

Living the spiritual life requires a childlike trust in God. Imagine yourself a child resting in the arms of a parent. Now allow yourself to become that child in relation to God. Envision yourself relaxing. Rest in God. This is infinitely more difficult than it sounds. Yet if you are someone who is weary of trying to be in control, this is a liberating position to take. How can you replace your anxieties with trust? This special kind of trust is not only a virtue—it is an art. It will take a lot of practice to live in this way of freedom.

. . . by prayer and petition, with thanksgiving, make your requests known to God. (v. 6)

A heart filled with awareness of reasons to be grateful is a superb guide for living. Even in the midst of life's disenchantments so many good things enrich us each day. Although we have been lavished with gifts and surrounded with beauty, it is easy to take all this goodness for granted. When we pray for our needs, then, let's pray with eyes open to the many reasons we have to be thankful. If we practice living with grateful hearts, we will become even more aware of daily blessings. Living with grateful hearts enables us to see with greater clarity our true needs. Pause for a few moments now. Take up your journal and compose a litany of gratitude. Let the memory of God's graciousness wash over you as you name your reasons for being thankful.

> *Then the peace of God that surpasses all understanding*
> *will guard your hearts and minds in Christ Jesus. (v. 7)*

The peace of God standing guard at our hearts and our minds is a comforting image—an uplifting promise. This promised peace will arrive at the door of our hearts if we are willing to practice the art of rejoicing always, trusting radically, living with grateful hearts, and letting our kindness overflow into the lives of others. Then comes the peace!

Even though Paul clearly states that the *peace of God* exceeds all understanding, being curious about this peace, I searched out other meanings and came across the word "ceasefire." Slightly amused, I lingered a while on the image of "ceasefire" standing guard at the door of my heart and mind. Although I find peace a more calming description, "ceasefire" certainly bears some truth and merits a few moments of consideration. It evokes the image of putting aside all barriers to reconciliation and understanding. In light of that harmonious glimpse of peace I would certainly invite "ceasefire" to keep vigil at the door of my heart.

Here, then, is your rule of life: your joy, which is the reverberation of God's life, will be visible to everyone. You freely allow kindness to blossom forth out of the ground of your being. Deep trust will replace your anxiety. A sincere gratitude will be the core of your prayer. The peace of Christ will stand guard over your heart.

Joy! Kindness! Trust! Gratitude! Peace! If you are open to claiming the power hidden in each of these virtues, your rule of life is ready to be your guide.

Reflection and Prayer

- Here is a summary of your *rule of life*: I will let *joy* be an echo of God's abiding presence in my life. I will attune my heart to the needs of others so that my *kindness* will blossom. My *trust* in the blessings of daily life will give me more power than my anxiety about daily life. Gratitude and *thankfulness* will be the center of all my prayer. I will invite the *peace* of Christ to stand guard over my heart.

- Use the summary above as points for your prayerful reflection.

- Take another look at the litany of gratitude you were asked to compose. Is there anything you want to add?

O God of Peace—God of Harmony,

I turn to you who are true and honorable, gracious and lovely. Give me the wisdom to welcome into the temple of my life the virtues of joy, kindness, trust, gratitude, and peace. Reveal to me my own open heart so that I may have the courage to let all that is good, worthy, and true take over my life. Send away all anxiety that keeps me focused on my fears. Deepen my desire to continue seeking you with all my heart. Never let me turn back to what might have been. Permit all that is good to flow out of my life and into the lives of others. **O you, who stand guard at the door of my heart, keep vigil with my desire for you.**

7. "Do Not Fret, It Only Leads to Evil"

Prayerfully read Psalm 37.

> *Do not be provoked by evildoers; do not envy those*
> *who do wrong. (v. 1)*

Psalm 37 is a powerful prayer of commitment. There is no looking back. You are to set your feet on the path that leads to justice—moving forward with a heart full of trust.

As we move into prayerful reflection on the theme of justice that this psalm offers us, I can imagine the questioning expressions and the angry thoughts that might surface. It is not an easy psalm to pray. Why shouldn't I be angry because of the wicked? My own emotions are stirred intensely as I try to enter into the hidden meaning of the psalmist's heart. However, on second thought, the meaning is not so hidden; it is right in my face and that is what I find offensive. Although in the second verse of the psalm, we are told that these evildoers will quickly wither away like dying vegetation, they never fade away fast enough for me. And what is all this talk about the gentle ones inheriting the land? It seems more accurate to say, "If you are gentle, the land will be taken from you." Let's be realistic and say, "The powerful shall inherit the land."

A friend once said to me, "Trying to pray with this psalm is like hugging a cactus." Her frustration is understandable. And yet, as I faithfully kept company with this particular Word of God, its good news began to settle like a song in my heart. In the midst of all the evil encircling me I look into the face of God and hear the story of life. God requires of us a tremendous trust in the truth that good will prevail. Perhaps we will even be given the grace to believe in the seed of goodness, lying uncared for in the hearts of the wicked.

> *Give up your anger, abandon your wrath;*
> *do not be provoked; it brings only harm. (v. 8)*

Abandoning your wrath and putting aside your anger is difficult yet admirable advice. I like the Grail translation of this psalm
verse, which reads, *"do not fret, it only leads to evil"*! These words
have become a personal mantra for me in some of the tough seasons of my life. Jesus was clear about the futility of fretting in
telling us that all of our worry and anxiety cannot add a single
day to our lives (Luke 12:25). And I, who spend a fair amount of
time fretting, suddenly realize that I am being called to be more
hopeful—less anxious.

As I am drawn deeper into the heart of this psalm's teaching, I
hear the promise that there is a future for the peaceful person. The
constant promise repeated throughout this psalm is that the land
will be a reward for the just. Thus the land becomes a symbol for
my prayer. The land remembers. It doesn't forget the sacred power
it contains. Through the rockiest of soil, life continues to lift up its
face. A land brutalized by war is still the womb of so much potential.

I reflect too on the ancient peoples whose lands we have con-
quered. Sometimes it seems as though their spirits still hover
around us—forgiving us, blessing us. Perhaps they are leading us
to the holy land of our own lives, where we will find the spiritual
powers we are tempted to ignore.

> *Turn from evil and do good,*
> *that you may inhabit the land forever.*
> *For the LORD loves justice and does not abandon the faithful.*
> *(vv. 27-28)*

This psalm is obviously a prayer that battles with good and
evil. It sings, with a passionate belief, the truth that good will

prevail. It calls us to discover and trust the land within—the land that remembers and knows more than we do. The *land within* is a place of peace where we are all one with God. The difficult part is that we are asked to discover this place of peace and hope right in the midst of the evil that surrounds us.

Yet, if we can be at peace in the promised land of the "deep self," we will be able to use that peace to help transform the world. To do this, we must experience and feel our anger. It is not possible to transform the world with our anger. The anger needs to be changed into love. To speak the truth with love is a huge challenge for most of us. We will probably be more successful in speaking the truth lovingly if we have worked through our anger in healthy ways. Being angry because of the injustice that is so prevalent in our society is both understandable and necessary. The grace we need is the ability to edit our anger, so that it can be useful in speaking our truth and doing God's work.

[T]hose at peace with God have a future. (v. 37)

In every age God sends us new poet-prophets to assist us in grasping ancient truths. If you treat yourself to the prophetic CD *Change Our Hearts*, by Rory Cooney, you can listen to the words of this awesome song: *"Do not fear to hope, though the wicked rage and rise. Our God sees not as we see; success is not the prize."*[4] Although we seem to live in a world where it is difficult to convince people that success is not the prize, those words are medicinal wisdom for me.

May the seed of hope in your promised land flourish and grow stronger each day, until that hope becomes your greatest prize.

Reflection and Prayer

- In the face of all the violence and injustice we live with, why does the seed of hope still have a place in your heart? Why do you not lose heart?

- My answer to that question is as follows: many good people still walk the face of this earth. New prophets are born every day. The bluebird continues to build her nest in the spring, and the daisies return in summer. People continue to reach out with incredible love to the less fortunate . . . and on and on and on. What about you? Why do you not despair?

- In one of your prayer periods bring to mind some of the reasons you are, at times, tempted to lose heart. Listing these in your journal might be helpful. Then in the face of these reasons to be discouraged, list some of the many reasons why your heart still knows joy.

O God of Hope and Transformation,

Lay your hand upon the people of this world who seem to have no conscience for doing right. Consider the ones whose hearts and minds are full of greed with no thought for the less fortunate. Through your transforming love, work miracles in their lives—miracles that will change their hearts. Lay your hand also upon all that is complacent in my life. Change my greed to generosity. Replace my anxiety with trust. We are your poet-prophets of today and we long to speak the truth with love. **Show us the path to your love.**

8. Before the Mountains Were Born

Prayerfully read Psalm 90.

> *Lord, you have been our refuge through all generations.*
> *Before the mountains were born,*
> *the earth and the world brought forth,*
> *from eternity to eternity you are God. (vv. 1-2)*

Eternity is a long, long time. Perhaps it is even what we might call a never-ending story. One of my earliest memories of theological reflection is sitting in our backyard when I was about ten years old pondering eternity. Try as I might, I just couldn't figure out how God could possibly have no beginning and no end. To no avail, I would try to think back as far as forever. It was a fascinating and exasperating exercise. I would finally surrender all efforts to solve this mystery and move on to more manageable pastimes.

Psalm 90 begins with my childhood quandary: "from eternity to eternity you are God." I smile as I recall author James Finley suggesting that *"when you try to figure out the unfigure-outable you get a headache."* A good observation! Better to take a deep breath and reach for the hand of mystery! There are incomprehensible mysteries in the heavens and the earth. From ancient times we have used stories, parables, poetry, and folk songs in our feeble yet loving attempts to touch the truth. In our biblical history we have cradled the unbelievable in our hearts and called it faith.

However, even in my grown-up years I still find both comforting and unfathomable the psalmist's assertion that we were sheltered in the mind and heart of God before the mountains were formed. I need the comfort of a simple faith in God's love for me.

I also need those vast, impenetrable mysteries drawing me into wistful longing for what I cannot reach on my own.

> *A thousand years in your eyes are merely a yesterday,*
> *But humans you return to dust, saying, "Return, you mortals!"*
> *(vv. 4, 3)*

Swiftly the tone of the psalm changes from consoling and encouraging to somber. We move from the reassuring reminder that God has been our refuge from all ages to the sober reality of the shortness of our lives. Suddenly we are invited to struggle with the eternity of forever in contrast to the brief, ephemeral nature of our lives. We who have made such a god of time must face its fleeting temperament.

Perhaps this seemingly harsh proclamation is, in reality, not such bitter news after all. Is it not an honest appraisal of our brief, time-bound days? Does not the Eternal One who cherished us in our coming cherish us in our going as well? We might fade away and wither like the grass, but have we not been tenderly held in the hands of God in the space between birth and death? Although it is true that, for God, a thousand years is a mere glimpse into our human history, I believe that brief glimpse is a glance of love. One moment of God's love is enough for our liberation. Perhaps it is sheer grace to be reminded that we arrived in love and depart in love. The space between our arrival and departure is life lived in love to the best of our ability.

> *You have kept our faults before you,*
> *our hidden sins exposed to your sight. (v. 8)*

Not only are we reminded that we, who have been in God's heart forever, will fade like the grasses of the field but now it is also announced that our sins are not hidden from the sight of the Creator. Although it may appear that the time has arrived when we should bow low with discouragement, I insist that even pondering God's anger can be healthy. The Lord knows our potential for good and wants us to be all we were created to be. Therefore, isn't it possible that God's anger flows from his love for us?

As I reflect on my own sinfulness dwelling alongside my desire for good, I am heartened with the memory of times when even God has a change of heart. The prophet Joel tells us, *"Perhaps [God] will again relent and leave behind him a blessing"* (Joel 2:14). I have experienced this many times. Even in the midst of my wrong choices, when faced with the discouragement of choosing my own will rather than the will of God, I stumble into blessings. God can allow good to flow even from our mistakes. Then, too, if I feel oppressed with the thought of God's anger, I can always find comfort in the arms of the divine by returning to the psalms: "This I know: God is on my side" (Ps 56:10).

Thus I begin to understand that even though the psalmist leads us on a journey where we must embrace our fragility, all this is for the purpose of helping us to gain wisdom of heart. It is in the midst of our daily struggles that we begin to see the face of the One who has sheltered us before the mountains were born.

So let us not look back with regret to that moment of being loved before the mountains were formed, as though it was only a fleeting, bittersweet moment. And let us not look forward, with fearful hesitancy, to the time when we will fade away like the grass. Rather, let us embrace the space between birth and death—that lovely place where, touched by grace, we live our lives each day joyfully committed to the present moment.

We end this psalm with a tone of trust, for surely it is a better prayer to ask for joy through all our days than to complain about the fleeting nature of our lives.

> *Fill us at daybreak with your love,*
> *that all our days we may sing for joy. (v. 14)*

Fearful and vulnerable moments in our lives can be transformed into cherished memories of times when we have been taught to call upon God's name. Daybreak is an appropriate metaphor. It points us toward the return of light and joy. We bring this reflection to a close with daybreak in our hearts.

Reflection and Prayer

- Spend some time abiding in each of these two moments: (a) the comfort of rejoicing in the truth that God has been a refuge for you before the mountains were born, and (b) the fragility of the truth that you will fade away like the grasses of the fields.

- Can you find consolation in both of these places?

O God of the Ages,

Before the mountains were born, you have been my shelter. You are my forever, my eternity. You knew me before I was formed in my mother's womb. And even now, you are my refuge and resting place. You are the answer to my eternal questions. You are the question to which my heart kneels down and waits in silence. O Holy Mystery, you are my mountain, my desert, my meadow. You are my daybreak and my nightfall. You are my waterfall of laughter, my stream of tears. Although my life will fade away like the grasses of the field, I am not afraid because your love is stronger than death. **O Holy Mystery, from eternity to eternity you are my God.**

Poetic Summary of Chapter Four

Don't Look Back

I love the plough that opens up the earth, lays bare the soil where seed can fall. It matters little that the widening wound of earth still hesitates, uncertain of the nutrients it has to offer falling seed. The seed is sown, the wound of earth closed up again. The broken soil becomes a womb, a sheltering tomb of life protecting what must die to live. We wait then for signs of life: the stem, the leaf, the bud, the fruit or vegetable to wend its way from dark to light. The image of the plough opening the soil to welcome seed offers us a metaphor for the human heart. The heart too must be prepared, readied to receive its daily seed. No more looking back!

I love the Word of God that pierces the human heart, lays bare the soul where seed can fall. The sower's passion invites the heart to receptivity. The sower looks not back to see if the heart is worthy. Sower and plough become one. With contemplative awareness they trust the widening wound of the opening heart. This laying bare the heart's good soil is a moment of readiness. She or he who receives the seed of the Word of God receives also the silence of the Word and waits to be transformed. No more looking back!

I love the disciple who allows the heart to be pierced. Obedient to the piercing Word and broken heart, the disciple learns to wait, trusting the Word to die and live within the heart's good soil. The disciple's heart becomes a sheltering womb and tomb for what must die to live. I love the one who is transformed into a disciple by surrendering to the Word of God. Rooted in obedience to the Word, there is no more looking back!

Chapter Five

Return
to Your Original Love

In the book of Revelation John is given specific messages for the seven churches of Asia. Each message begins with an affirmation and ends with a challenge or warning. His message to the church of Ephesus seems to have been written just for me. I like both the affirmation and the challenge.

My paraphrased version goes something like this: I have noticed that you are responsible and hardworking; you are conscientious about your ministry. I am aware that you try to root out evil with good. You have been faithful. You have not abandoned my message even in times of weariness. Nevertheless, I hold this against you: you have fallen away from your original love (Rev 2:4).

How easy it is to allow the flame of our early devotion to be snuffed out because of busyness and deadlines. In my personal daily living I often find myself longing for those "in the beginning" times. I am almost always more faithful *in the beginning.* In the beginning of any season I feel more awake; I live with more dedication and enthusiasm.

Even the seasons receive my wholehearted attention when they first arrive. Autumn, winter, spring, and summer awaken the child in me. I approach each new season with awe. In the prayerful seasons of Advent and Lent I glow with hopeful anticipation and gratitude for being offered new ways to grow spiritually. These seasons attract me and stir up what has grown stale in my life. But then something happens! The newness wears off and my wonderful "in the beginning" dries up like a brook in summer's heat.

We see this in some marriages. People who fall passionately in love soon fall out of love. What happens? Where does that love go? Friendship is another sacrament that often suffers from neglect; and neglect can eventually lead to death. You can probably come up with many examples in your own life—examples of something once precious that has died.

My first fervor is even observed in my journal writing. When I begin a new journal, the first twenty pages or so are very legible. But then something happens and I go back to my original scribble as I lose my original fervor. It is obvious that my busyness begins to overshadow my original joy in prayerful journaling.

When I attend a retreat or go away for personal time for spiritual renewal, I often return home with a wonderful sense of renewed energy and even transformation. Yet, how quickly my "mountaintop" experience falls away! Does my experience resonate, in any way, with you? Have you experienced this falling away from your original love?

You have come to the last chapter of *Abide*, "Return to Your Original Love." This is your "return to the basics" chapter. Take some time to seriously pray with, and evaluate, some of the first loves of your life. Reflect on your relationship with God. Has it grown stale? Has your faithfulness to prayer diminished? Has your work stolen your heart? How can you return to your original love? How can you learn to abide? How do you need to keep vigil? Has something happened to your good zeal of earlier years?

1. United In Purpose

Prayerfully read 1 Corinthians 3:1-25.

> *According to the grace of God given to me,*
> *like a wise master builder I laid a foundation,*
> *and another is building upon it. (v. 10)*

Our reflection begins with Paul pleading with the church in Corinth to listen to one another and become united in a single purpose. The fact that he is preaching these words suggests that Paul has been informed of disharmony and divisions in the community. He has heard about their quarreling. The controversy involved the issue of teachers. Some were saying they were disciples of Paul, some Apollos. Others claimed to belong to Cephas, still others to Christ. Paul's response to all this bickering was that they should make every effort to become united in mind and purpose. They are to return to their original love and embrace again the moment they became one in Christ Jesus.

The wrangling among the Corinthians sounds vaguely familiar. In many of our Christian circles today there are heated disputes about how to live out the truths of the Gospel. At times we have an elitist attitude about teachers and schools of spirituality. Today you might hear, "I belong to Merton; I belong to Francis, Ignatius of Loyola, or Mother Teresa. I am a charismatic. I am contemplative, or monastic. I am a social justice activist. I am a Christian feminist."

Thus the same question that Paul put to the Corinthians could be asked of us today. Is Christ divided? Isn't it union with Christ that we are all seeking? Is that not our original intent? The heart of Paul's mission was to illumine the Word of God. The challenging Gospel

Paul proclaimed was then, and still is today, a message that sounds like folly to those who have bought into the wisdom of this world.

When we see the heartbreaking violence and evils enacted by well-educated and intelligent people in our world today, it does seem that the so-called *wisdom of this world* is absurdity. We certainly are not united in purpose. We are far from putting on *the mind of Christ*.

What kind of transformation needs to take place in our lives in order for us to live without divisions? Recently I read a story that described three monks who lived together in perfect harmony. How was this possible? Each one was compassionately concerned about the good of the other. Rather than focusing on his or her individual desires, each tried to discern the good of "the other."

From this little story I gleaned a bit of insight into what might be considered a universal flaw in human beings. It has something to do with wanting our own way, or perhaps, believing that *our way* is God's way. In the prologue to his Rule for monks, St. Benedict touches on this defect when he says, "This message of mine is for you, then, *if you are ready to give up your own will*" (v. 3). Oh, how I rebelled at those words as a novice in monastic life! The struggle to give up my own will is still one of my crosses.

Of course you might object; isn't it dangerous to give your will over to another? Doesn't this way of living sound like the beginnings of a cult? Indeed it does, and that is precisely why I prefer to put the emphasis on being united in a common purpose rather than that of becoming one mind and one heart. I don't know if it is possible to become one mind and one heart. Yet if I am willing to drop little pieces of "my way" in order to focus on "our way," then I am, in some small way, giving up my own will.

The story of the three monks living together in harmony inspired me to reflect on my own crosses. I know from personal experience that clinging to my own way is a cross that is not redemptive. Many of the crosses we choose to carry are not redeeming. To name just a few: living with resentment, withholding forgiveness, needing to be in control, being unwilling to learn from others, selfishly demanding my own way, remaining imprisoned in addictive ways of living. It takes a certain amount of maturity to even notice that we are carrying a cross of our creation—carved out of our own foolishness. To be caught up in our tiny world, thinking only of our wants and needs, with hearts closed to others, is perhaps the greatest of unredemptive crosses. In this way of living there is no room for love, and life without love is a heavy cross to carry.

There is another kind of cross, though. It is the cross of our salvation. We meditate on this cross when, with Paul, we preach Christ crucified—Christ desiring not his own way but wanting only our good. The pain that comes from carrying this cross is redemptive because it is born out of love. Someone said to me once, "I'm in pain but I'm not suffering." Although she was in much physical pain, her attitude was one of acceptance. She was receiving the pain rather than fighting it. She was carrying a cross that was redemptive.

> *For the wisdom of this world is foolishness in the eyes of God.*
> *(v. 19)*

The idea of a cross that redeems is total absurdity to those who are wise by the world's standards. But to those who are *experiencing salvation*, the cross is the *power* and wisdom of Christ. That is Paul's message not only to the Corinthians but also to you and me.

When Paul speaks of those who are *experiencing salvation*, he is suggesting that salvation is a process. Paul sees salvation as a gift that we are constantly receiving if we choose to live in the power and wisdom of God and if we are resolved to put on the mind of Christ.

Novelist Ella Cara Deloria[1] tells a story that beautifully depicts how the cross became an experience of salvation for a tribe of Dakota Indians. When one of the young males in the tribe is murdered, the infuriated kinsfolk gather to decide how to settle the ordeal. The elder in the tribe listens quietly to the angry debate. Eventually he speaks difficult words of wisdom. He tells them that he understands their rage and their desire to kill the murderer. *"However," he suggests, "there is a better way—and that the fire of hate may not burn on in his heart or in ours, we shall take that better way."*

The elder tells the relatives to go home and bring their most prized possession as a gift for the murderer. In giving him these gifts they are to make of him their relative in place of the one who has been killed. *"Was the dead man your brother? Then this man shall be your brother. Was he your uncle? Or, your cousin? As for me," the elder says, "the dead was my nephew. Therefore, his slayer shall be my nephew. From now on he shall be one of us. We shall regard him as though he were our dead kinsman returned to us."* And so the tribe learned that although it is easy to fight violence with violence, it is nobler to forgive.

The slayer was brought into the tipi, presented the gifts, offered the peace pipe, and told that from this day on the love and compassion they once had for their dead brother would now be his. Tears flowed from the murderer's eyes. A great silence fell upon the community. Words were not needed. Both he and his tribe were experiencing salvation. This story is an example of the foolishness of God that is wiser than human wisdom.

Meditate on this story. Recall living memories from your life when a painful and unwanted cross suddenly became an experience of salvation for you.

Reflection and Prayer

- Does your spiritual practice include Paul's dream for us to be united in a common purpose? How is this reflected in your daily life?

- Name some of your daily personal crosses that are redemptive; then think of others that are not redemptive. How might you work with those unredemptive crosses to bring about changes that will align your will with the will of God?

- Is giving up your own will a part of your spiritual practice? Does living in such a manner that you are always thinking of "the other's" good sound attractive to you?

- Does the story of forgiveness in this reflection annoy you or inspire you?

O Love Divine, All Loves Excelling,

It is love we need. Your intent has always been to gather us together as one people. How difficult it is for us to have one mind and one heart. Look upon our hearts and minds so scattered and divided in their many loves. Plant in each of us a desire to be united with Jesus in a common purpose. Make our longing for unity deeper than our longing to do our own will. Give us a heart for others. Give us the signs, the wisdom, and the love we need to learn the art of forgiveness, which is really the art of loving. In the name of Jesus we pray. **Amen.**

2. "Chosen and Precious"

Prayerfully read 1 Peter 2:1-10.

[L]ike newborn infants, long for pure spiritual milk. (v. 2)

Milk is not among my favorite drinks, thus the request to have a yen for the milk of my infant days is not all that attractive to me. In praying with this Scripture text, however, it occurred to me how unusual it is for babies to turn away from milk. As infants, we were eager for milk. It was our original nourishment. Later in life we may have made the choice to delete it from our diet but it was our first drink. It satisfied our early hunger cries.

As my dry bones begin speaking to me I am listening anew to the good news of milk. Calcium becomes a blessing as I search for foods rich in this necessary mineral. In telling us to be as eager for milk as newborn infants, Peter is asking us to return to our beginnings. Look back to some of your original sources of nourishment. The food for which our physical bodies crave is an excellent metaphor for our spiritual hungers. Taste is one of the five senses in which most of us take pleasure. Over the years we grow in awareness that certain foods, although pleasing to our taste buds, are not healthy for us. They taste good but they don't really nourish us. When I think back to my early life on my childhood farm, I remember gardens full of fresh vegetables. Although I didn't always appreciate those vegetables as a child, I now realize just what a treasure the earth was offering me. Learning how to prepare and to season vegetables in a way that enhances the flavor is an art. Learning how to serve spiritual food is also an art.

[F]or you have tasted that the Lord is good. (v. 3)

We develop a taste for the spiritual according to how it is presented to us. Whether the Lord tastes good probably depends on how God has been revealed to us in our early years. If our experience of God consisted of a list of rules and pat answers to memorize, the Lord may not have tasted very sweet. So you see, it does depend on how the Lord is served. Seasoning is important to bring out the flavor in spiritual food just as it is in physical food.

When Peter tells us that we have *already tasted the goodness of the Lord*, he is referring to the beginning of our relationship with Jesus. As we mature in our faith life, relationships change and grow more intimate. No matter what our age is now, in some small way, we have probably grown away from the intimate beginnings of our early faith experience. Take a few moments to reflect on your original love of God. Or, you might reflect on a time in your life when your devotion to the things that really matter seemed more vibrant. Spend time discerning what spiritual gifts need to be restored in your life.

Is there anything you would like to call back into your consciousness? Has something that once nourished you gotten lost in the busyness of daily living? A childlike spirit? An openness to learning? A natural simplicity? A nurturing relationship? Quality time for prayer and study? What spiritual calcium is needed to help you build a strong foundation?

If you have neglected caring for your body, it may be too late to totally remedy the situation. It is never too late, though, to take a new look at your spiritual health. Those original moments of nourishments to which we are invited to return have none of the harshness of the things we are asked to strip away: malice and deceit, insincerity, envy, and slander. Obviously, these do not nourish the soul. They will not assist us on the road to holiness and happiness.

Come to him, a living stone, rejected by human beings
but chosen and precious in the sight of God. (v. 4)

Do you feel chosen? Do you feel precious? Peter invites us to come to the *living stone* that was rejected by the establishment yet chosen as the cornerstone. This living stone is Jesus, who cements the church together through his life, death, and resurrection.

Through the Spirit of Jesus each of us is carved into a living stone. We are a priestly people. We too offer the sacrifice of our lives for the transformation of the world at the altar of daily life. If we allow this truth to rise in our consciousness, it will permeate our entire lives until we become a blessing, another Christ for our world.

Even in our day, we have examples of living stones that have been rejected by the system. Their memory lives on as bright lights of encouragement for us. To name just a few: Oscar Romero, Stanley Rother, Sr. Ita Ford and her companions. These brothers and sisters listened to the call of Jesus to stand beside the poor and oppressed. In doing so, they sacrificed their lives and were elevated to the ranks of the living stones that hold the church together.

Those of us whose life-offering seems less dramatic need not be discouraged. There is a daily dying that makes each of us, in our own unique way, a living stone. We too support the church by giving it vitality and cementing it together by the holiness of our lives.

Proclaim the praises of the One who summoned you
out of darkness into wondrous light. (see v. 9)

Darkness has many faces. The darkness we have been called out of still appears among us in various forms. It could be the darkness of negativity, selfish gain, oppression, misused power, or despair. It might emerge in the guise of hostility, prejudice, and indifference. It could be any of the vices Peter asked us to strip away as we turn eagerly to the things that nourish us.

God's marvelous light empowers us as we move out of the darkness that keeps us trapped in our immaturity. We taste, in new ways, that the Lord is good. We experience the joy of being chosen and claimed as God's own possession.

These teachings from the First Letter of Peter are about a renewal of our spiritual health. At this time when many of us look toward alternative medicines and holistic ways of dealing with illnesses, we are invited to add to that list a return to the pure milk of the spirit.

Reflection and Prayer

- How were you spiritually nourished as a child? as a young adult? Are there any spiritual practices to which you would like to return?

- What is your understanding of holiness? Do you see yourself giving the church vitality by the holiness of your life?

- Many questions were asked in this reflection. Return to those questions and spend time praying with them.

Chosen and Precious One,

Choose me again. Enable me to believe in the part of myself that is precious. Teach me the art of flavoring the world with goodness. Make me one of your living stones. Assist me in stripping away all the things that obscure the truth of my relationship with Christ. Encourage me to choose spiritual foods that feed my hunger for you. Turn my face away from the kind of darkness that hides the light of your presence. I too am chosen and precious. May the world be blessed because of my faithfulness to your presence in my life. **Amen, Amen.**

3. Called to Freedom

Prayerfully read Galatians 5.

> *For freedom Christ set us free; so stand firm*
> *and do not submit again to the yoke of slavery. (v. 1)*

In a world where so many people do not experience freedom, what can we say about being free? What does it mean to be free? Surely freedom is more than not living in prison, just as peace is not necessarily the absence of war.

In the fifth chapter of Galatians Paul shares some valuable insights about freedom. We are to live in such a manner that it will be obvious that we are following the Spirit's lead. The Spirit is to be our dance partner leading us into a life of faith in Christ. More powerful than any law, the Spirit leads us into the freedom of the children of God (Rom 8:21). This freedom is not an invitation to self-indulgence. Rather it is an invitation that can be accepted only by those persons who are mature enough to follow the Spirit's lead. Only a deeply discerning heart can give birth to a properly formed conscience. Thus "freedom isn't free." Hours of prayer, study, and practice are required to gain the maturity needed to live in the Spirit. Freedom does not mean just doing what we want to do.

On the other hand, if our wills are aligned with the will of God, we will be free to do what we want. For having risen above the law, our desire will always be for the greater good.

It is easy to feel righteous about ourselves because we have kept all the laws. Such an attitude, however, is reminiscent of the Pharisee and publican of the gospels. It lacks humility. Proud that we have kept all the laws, we tend to forget that true holiness cannot be achieved by mere performance of religious duties. Paul reminds us that if we live with this attitude, we are severing ourselves from Christ. He wants us to remember that it is the Spirit, not the law, that is to be the central focus of our lives.

The freedom that Christ leads us into does not require circumcision. In Romans 2:28-29 Paul speaks of a circumcision of the heart, which suggests a transformative process that frees us from legalism, and that ushers us into a new creation—the life of the Spirit.

It is always love that must govern the actions of those who have accepted Christ into their lives. There are ways of living that do not exemplify the life of a Christian. In verses 19-21 Paul lists these enemies of the spiritual life—cravings of the flesh, he calls them. These enticements are, in reality, the shadow side of the true self. They do not depict our true identities: temples of the Holy Spirit, created in the divine image. When we are in the midst of these cravings, we cannot see the harm they do. A story exemplifying this was recently shared with me by a friend. After explaining to a child that some of her favorite foods are not good for her, the child replies, "but I can't see them being bad for me." This is exactly the case. We cannot see the things that are harming us at the moment, but later our unhealthy patterns catch up to us. Paul knows this and tries to help us understand what our lives could be, if we remain open to God's love flowing freely through our being.

In the *fruits of the Spirit* (vv. 22-23), we are offered a more accurate portrait of the person whom we can become when we allow the Spirit to be our dance partner. We dream of and imagine a day when we will be a reservoir of "love, joy, peace, patience, kindness, generosity, faithfulness, gentleness, self-control." As you reflect on the *fruits of the Spirit*, take note of what a wondrous guide these virtues would be for an examination of conscience in preparation for the sacrament of reconciliation. As for the vices, these are part of your shadow self. There is gold in the shadow. All that rage and idolatry, the dissension, rivalries, jealousy, envy, and lust (vv. 19-21) have another side that needs to be understood. We must look beyond these actions to the gift waiting in the shadows. There in the shadows we will find a truer version of ourselves—clothed in the virtues.

Here are some points for your consideration as you pray with the fruits of the Spirit.

- *Joy:* When we remember that joy is God living at the very core of our beings, we will learn that joy can live in the midst of great sorrow.

- *Peace:* Are you ready to take a vow of nonviolence, including your thoughts?

- *Patience:* Think of the last time when you were really impatient with yourself or others. What was the underlying cause of your impatience?

- *Kindness:* What is your latest memory of a kindness done for you? When we are grateful for such moments, our gratitude can draw forth from us amazing kindnesses.

- *Generosity:* Which one of these is the greatest challenge to your generosity: your time, your possessions, your money, or your talents?

- *Faith:* If you leapt into the waters of your faith, how deep would you go?

- *Self-control:* On the days when you appear to have no self-control, when you reach out for things that are unhealthy, could it be God for whom you are searching?

- *Love:* Love crowns them all. Saint John of the Cross tells us that in the evening of our lives we will be judged on love. At the end of this day, check your heart. How well have you loved?

Reflection and Prayer

- Can you envision the Spirit being your dance partner? Imagine, too, how your life would be different if this were the case. Let it be!

- Take a walk with each of the fruits of the Spirit this week. This would be a wonderful exercise to use on a labyrinth walk if one is available.

O Spirit of the Living God,

Free me! Free me from my self-made prison. Abide in me! I want to be your dwelling place. Entice me! Lure me back to my original love. Support me! Align me with the will of God! Purify me! Breathe into the tightly closed places of my life. Adorn me! Robe me with the fruits of the spirit of Jesus. Guide me! Lead me in the footsteps of Jesus. Anoint me! Transform my prison into a temple of your glory. **O Spirit of the Living God, abide in me.**

4. A Season of Forgiveness

Prayerfully read Genesis 33.

> *Have you known a season of forgiveness?*
> *Chains that bound you fell away.*
> *You became a household of love*
> *for someone waiting*
> *on the doorstep of your heart.*

Today we are going to keep company with Jacob as he makes his journey toward reconciliation with his brother Esau. Spend some time with the Jacob and Esau story. Try to remember moments in your own life when you, like Jacob, were in need of forgiveness. Ponder as well moments when, like Esau, you had an opportunity to forgive someone. Our ability to forgive is, perhaps, one of our most Godlike qualities.

A sad story that remains in my memory is that of a man at his brother's deathbed, begging forgiveness and receiving nothing more than an empty, bitter stare. That empty, bitter stare must have come from a heart that simply could not open. Although we do not understand the mystery of that closed heart, we can recognize that the unforgiven brother is given an opportunity to forgive the unforgiveness.

Another story lingers in my memory. Back in the sixties, during the civil rights movement, I sat on the porch of an elderly woman in an inner-city parish. I was deeply moved as she talked about her son who had been murdered. "Not a day goes by," she said, "when tears don't come." "But then one day," she explained, "another kind of tear rolled down my cheek. It was a tear for the one who murdered my son and the terrible burden he has to carry through life. That new tear washed away chains that were binding me. It was a tear that set me free and helped me to forgive."

We have here two very different stories. In the first story a person who is begging for forgiveness doesn't receive it. In the second story an unknown person, out there somewhere, receives forgiveness that he didn't even ask for. Did the forgiveness change his heart? We really don't know. The woman offering her gift of forgiveness will probably never know if her son's murderer repented. What she does know is that the freedom she experienced in being able to forgive lifted a burden and "set her free."

Now that we have considered both the challenge and joy of forgiveness, we return to Jacob and his movement toward reconciliation. After a night of struggle with a divine messenger (Gen 32:23-33), Jacob moves forward with his new name and his holy limp. Chapter 33 of Genesis begins with these words: *"Jacob looked up and saw Esau coming, accompanied by four hundred men."* There is heaviness in these words. It is easy for us to paint a picture of the scene. We can well imagine what Jacob is feeling.

As we observe Jacob's maneuvers in arranging his nomadic household for this meeting with Esau, we readily discern that his new name hadn't put him totally at ease with this venture. He carries his hope, like a tiny jewel, hidden away in an overcautious heart because he is uncertain about what he will find in the heart of Esau.

Thus, to protect what is most precious to him, Jacob places Rachel and Joseph at the end of the procession. Jacob then moves toward Esau with seven ritual bowings.

The tender scene of his brother, in tears, running to meet him and embracing him, reveals to us something of the cathartic experience that is taking place in Esau's heart. With Esau's loving welcome it might appear that the gifts sent ahead for appeasement were unnecessary. This *sending forth of gifts*, however, was a vital purification act for Jacob's soul. In this action we sense a dramatic statement of Jacob's realization that he had sinned against his brother. As this beautiful season of forgiveness blossoms, Jacob is overcome with the loving kindness with which he has been received. His words to Esau are filled with humility: *"to come into your presence is for me like coming into the presence of God, now that you have received me so kindly"* (v. 10).

This inspiring reunion of the two brothers provides wonderful material for our prayer. Hold up this event against your own life to see what questions or insights emerge for your personal reflection.

Reflection and Prayer

- Put yourself in Jacob's heart. Try to experience his desire to be forgiven as well as his uncertainty and fear.

- Become Esau for awhile. Live in his mind and heart. Imagine his feelings. Relive the moment of reunion.

- Think of a time in your life when you needed to forgive someone. Pray for that person. Is there anything that is unfinished between the two of you?

- Is there anyone whose forgiveness you need to experience? What would it cost you in terms of time, pride, or love to complete the process of forgiveness?

Gracious Guide on All Our Journeys,

Be with the Esau-and-Jacobs of this world. Empower them to find their hearts of flesh, their holy limp, and their new names as they continue on their individual pilgrimages of reconciliation. Move into my heart-space and speak to me of compassionate loving. The road to forgiveness is so challenging. Encourage me. Support me. Affirm me. I invite into the household of my love all those whom I struggle to forgive. (Mention names.) **O God of so much mercy, teach me vulnerability.**

5. How Dear You Are!

Prayerfully read 1 Thessalonians 1 and 2.

> *We give thanks to God always for all of you,*
> *remembering you in our prayers, unceasingly*
> *calling to mind your work of faith and labor of love. (1:2-3)*

In these two short chapters to the Thessalonians it is obvious that Paul holds dear this community of faith and yearns to keep close connection to them. He wants these followers of Jesus to live in such a way that they might become an example to other Gentiles. What is so attractive about this letter is how pastoral it is; no authoritarian tone is present. The loving concern and devotion of Paul's words to these disciples is remarkably tender. It is a quality that those among us who proclaim the Good News to others might hope to imitate.

> *You too are disciples who have been taught by others. Who have*
> *been your teachers and mentors in learning to love the Word*
> *of God? Invite them into your soul's memory. Pray for these*
> *teachers and thank them if possible.*

Paul's expression is one of delight and passion as he writes to the community of converts in Thessalonica. His joy overflows as he learns about their labor of love and he wants them to remember the truth that they have been chosen and set apart for God's service. The Word they received was empowered by the Holy Spirit. As we look at our own evolving relationship with Jesus, we might want to examine our hearts concerning this question: how have we turned from idols to serve the living God?

What idols do you still juggle in your personal life?
Do you feel chosen? When you read the words of Scripture,
do you allow yourself to experience
the power of the Holy Spirit?

In praying with these Scripture passages it is heart-stirring to see the enthusiasm with which Paul attempts to encourage, support, and affirm his disciples. It is no secret that Paul and his colleagues have taken great risks and endured harassment in offering the Word of God to others. In spite of the suffering they experienced, they were filled with loving boldness. They were impelled to continue proclaiming the Gospel in the face of opposition. They were zealous in preaching because they felt passionate about being entrusted with the sacred message. They came not with mandates but as devoted parents nurturing their children.

Can you identify with Paul's great passion
for the Word of God?
Are you willing to take to heart the people
to whom you minister?
Do you ever feel on fire
when you offer the Word of God to others?
How would your ministry change
if you experienced feeling utterly entrusted
with the Word of God?

Sadly the beauty of this pastoral gem has been marred because of a rather vicious anti-Semitic passage that was likely inserted in Paul's letter at a later date and numbered as 1 Thessalonians 2:13-16. Yet in Paul's letter to the Romans (3:9-11), he emphatically stresses that all are under the dominion of sin. All are guilty. We must all take responsibility for the sin that is ours. We ought not to lay blame for the death of Jesus on any one group of people. Blaming others is never a responsible way of living and it is certainly not conducive to the Christian way of life.

In rereading these first two letters to the Thessalonians I am moved by Paul's obvious intent toward encouragement. I have no doubt that these encouraging words for the Thessalonians are also intended for struggling Christians of today. To summarize the message gleaned from these directives given to first-century Christians, here is my paraphrase of Paul's message. As you read these words try to imagine that your present-day teachers are speaking to you today in this twenty-first century.

Our hearts are stirred in memory of all of you who struggle to live a Christian life. With the tenderness of a loving mother and father we have nurtured you with truth. Your faithful reception to the Word of God fills us with a joyful gratitude. With jubilation we behold your abiding love and constant hope. Your faith in the midst of trials is astounding. Truly you have understood that the words given to you are filled with the power of the Holy Spirit. You have received these words with joy and shared them with enthusiasm.

If you remember nothing else of the Good News that has been proclaimed to you, remember this: You are dear—dear to God and to the ones who have given you these words of life. You are our glory and joy. We sing praises before God because of you. The Word of God has been entrusted to you and you have proved yourselves worthy of that trust. Continue to live anointed with the Word of God. Never forget how dear you are.

Reflection and Prayer

- Are you able to set aside some time each day to truly abide with the Word of God in Scripture? Do you notice a difference in the way you relate to others when you are able to be faithful to *lectio divina*?

- When you read Scripture with an open heart, attentive to this inspired Word of God, you will often receive glimpses of the truth that you are dear and beloved in God's eyes. Can you allow yourself to feel dear?

O Endearing Spirit of the Holy One,

How tenderly you have enfolded me in God's creative love throughout the years! Continue to set your seal of love upon my heart. Open my eyes to see the many ways I am cherished and held dear by my loving Creator. Renew my desire to put down deep roots into the Word of God. Fulfill my yearning to grow strong in my faith by grounding me in Sacred Scripture. Bless the many holy guides who have given so much of their time for the enrichment of my spiritual life. Bless too all those who have come to know you through my simple guidance. May this marvelous exchange of the Word of God among one another help each of us to understand how dear we are. **O Endearing One, enable us to be drawn to the things that really matter.**

6. Jesus Stopped

Prayerfully read Mark 10:46-52.
(Put yourself in each of the scenes from this gospel.)

Bartimaeus, a blind man, . . . sat by the roadside begging. (v. 46)

The blind beggar sitting by the roadside was doing what all beggars do—begging. He was making known that he needed something to sustain him. Something to keep him alive and give him hope! Something to heal and comfort him! Most of us can probably relate to that beggar. Our eyes may not be blind but we often wear blinders. We too are lacking in sight. Or, perhaps, we are lacking insight! How healthy are the eyes of your heart? If you had an opportunity to ask Jesus for greater sight, for what would you ask? What is missing in your life? What aren't you seeing? How do you need to return to your original love? It may be something in your personal life or it may relate to the needs of others. Many voices are crying out. There is so much injustice that needs our attention. What do you need to see? Where do you need greater clarity? How often do you find yourself crying out to the Lord in your need?

On hearing that it was Jesus of Nazareth, he began to cry out.
(v. 47)

Each time we ask Jesus for a blessing, we are, in some way, asking ourselves for that same blessing. Before dismissing that statement as irrelevant, give it serious consideration. When you ask, in prayer, for the assistance you need, it would be good for you to look into your heart to see if there is something you might do to help answer your own prayer. When we pray with sincerity, we become more aware of what is lacking in our lives. We ask for graces for ourselves and for others. Sometimes we have to bring these needs not just to God but also to people who are in a position to help make changes that will bring a better quality of life to others. We ask our senators and congresspersons, our mayors and city council members. We ask our fellow citizens. We, like the blind beggar, cry out to someone more powerful than ourselves, trying to get our needs heard. There are also times when we are told to be quiet.

And many rebuked him, telling him to be silent. (v. 48)

Peace activists come to my mind in this regard. They appear to be seeing with the eyes of Jesus. Yet how often they have been rebuked, called unpatriotic, and told to be silent. People who have taken a stand on issues of justice and peace have probably experienced being told to stay in their place. If we go out to feed the hungry, we are extolled, but if we question the system that is keeping them hungry, we become suspect. When the blind man is told to be quiet, however, he calls out even louder. Perhaps there is a lesson we can learn from this blind beggar.

Jesus stopped and said, "Call him." (v. 49)

When Jesus heard the pleading and persistent cry of the beggar, he stopped. Most of us find stopping and interrupting our schedules difficult. It is not easy for us to stop before we are finished with our project. In a poetic reflection written about Bartimaeus, the author focuses her entire meditation on these two words: *"Jesus stopped."* Although I have often used this Scripture passage for my *lectio*, until I read Janice Stanton's reflection, I had never singled out those two words with such significance. Jesus had to stop; he had to interrupt his journey so that he could give his full attention to the one who was calling his name. Do we know when to stop? Take a look at your schedules, your opinions, your ideas, your attitudes. How do you need to stop and listen to your life? It is impossible to be truly present to another person while clinging to your own agenda. Stop and hear the cries of the poor. Stop and ask yourself some questions. Is there anything I need to see in a different light? How do I hear the voice of Jesus in my life?

Take courage; get up, he is calling you. (v. 49)

To "take courage" means to "take heart." Every time you pray, you have the opportunity of hearing the voice of the Beloved. To hear the intimacy of that voice, though, you will need to stop. Stop the words. Stop praying. Just listen. We, like the blind beggar, can know the joy of hearing the voice of Jesus saying to us, Take heart! Be encouraged! Be refreshed! Be restored!

This is the kind of Good News we all yearn to hear. Someone broadcasting that we are about to be given a new heart, a new lease on life! We only have to stop, as the one who is about to heal us has stopped, and let it be done to us.

He threw aside his cloak, sprang up, and came to Jesus. (v. 50)

This indeed is a dance of joy. The throwing aside his cloak suggests a new freedom. It is a dance of joy. Is there anything I need to rid myself of before I can come, in faith, to Jesus? The blind man comes to Jesus unencumbered. He has taken the risk, at the price of ridicule, to call out the holy name. His action of throwing aside his cloak suggests a readiness for the big question, "What do you want me to do for you?" If you should hear—in the middle of your prayer, in the silence of your heart—that question being asked of you, what would your answer be? What gift do you long for? How do you need your sight restored? Do you want your insight to be deeper? Are you willing to let the blinders that keep you from a more reflective kind of seeing fall away? The blind beggar cast off his cloak. What do you need to cast off?

Could it be fear? or greed? perhaps excessive love of power or possessions? indifference? apathy? prejudice, distrust, cynicism? What are you willing to cast off? What are the veils that need to fall away so that you can see who you truly are? Do you want to be healed of all that prevents you from seeing with clarity? Take these questions to your prayer. Invite the blind beggar of yourself into your own heart. Is anyone calling out your name? This is your week to *stop and listen*. This is the time to return to your original love so that your dance of life may be more graceful.

Reflection and Prayer

- Contemplate the invitation to stop. Today and in the days that follow *watch yourself live.* Be on the lookout for opportunities to pause. These moments of pausing may be invitations to pray about your own dance of life. Or, they may be opportunities for you to reach out to someone who needs to take heart.

- Read the reflection on the blind beggar again. Highlight the questions asked and spend time listening to those questions.

O Healing Eye of God,

In this gracious moment of prayer I sense you pausing as you gaze into the center of my soul, asking, what do you want me to do for you? I too pause, wondering what is really essential in my life. Where do I need your therapeutic touch? Where do I need your healing breath? Following your gaze into my soul, I see all of the undanced dances of my life. I see the love I've withheld, the life I've not lived, the creativity that has grown stale from idle existing instead of vibrant living. I recall St. Irenaeus suggesting that when I live fully, I add to your glory and I cry out to you with hesitant hope. O God of Life, I want to live! I want to live so fully that I become another Christ. I want to love as you love. I want to see as you see. Thank you for stopping in my life today. Thank you for your penetrating gaze that has opened my closed eyes. I want to see myself living fully. I want your dance of life to be my own. I want to live! **O Healing Eye of God, abide in me!**

7. Somewhere In You Lives a Child

Prayerfully read Mark 10:13-16 and Luke 10:21-22.

> *[W]hoever does not accept the kingdom of God*
> *like a child will not enter it. (Mark 10:15)*

Children are the world's most precious resource, our hope for the future. They carry within their young souls the seed of new dreams for a world in so much need of healing. The child is fresh, innocent, curious, spontaneous, eager, natural, vulnerable, playful, full of laughter, tears, and dreams! Children are still able to be delighted in gifts without price tags: a penny, a colored stone, a feather, seashells, falling leaves, soap bubbles, clouds! Children have not learned how to say, I'm too busy to play. They usually don't try to edit their tears. These are the ones Jesus says we must become like if we are to enter the kingdom of heaven.

I am mentioning all of these wonderful traits of children with a bit of reluctance.

At a confirmation retreat I was leading a few years ago, I read this text from Mark and asked the young participants what they had lost from childhood that they wished could be restored. I was amazed at how many of them answered INNOCENCE. As our discussion continued it occurred to me that a great sadness in today's society is that we do not allow our children to remain children. Just as we force-feed animals in crowded pens allowing them no natural space in which to grow, thinking only in utilitarian terms of how quickly they can serve our needs, so too we hurriedly change children into little adults. But they aren't adults and somewhere inside each young person there is that child crying to be freed. Those of us who are no longer young can also hear that caged child asking to be set free.

In Jesus' blessing of children we find a visible reminder of the holiness of the child, still fresh from the womb, close to the source of life. How can we keep from spoiling them, harming and starving them, abusing and neglecting them? How can we keep from turning them into little adults before they are ready? As we reflect on the precious gift of young life, let's take to heart these words of Jesus: *"Let the children come to me; do not prevent them, for the kingdom of God belongs to such as these"* (Mark 10:14).

The child that Nikos Kazantzakis describes in his book *Report to Greco* is the kind of child I envision surrounding Jesus and approaching him to be blessed.

> I remember frequently sitting on the doorstep of our home when the sun was blazing, the air on fire, grapes being trodden in a large house in the neighborhood, the world fragrant with must. Shutting my eyes contentedly, I used to hold out my palms and wait. God always came—as long as I remained a child. He never deceived me—He always came, a child just like myself, and deposited his toys in my hands: sun, moon, wind. "They're gifts," he said, "They're gifts. Play with them. I have lots more." I would open my eyes. God would vanish, but His toys would remain in my hands.[2]

This kind of child can still be found in our world. The lost innocence that the confirmation class voiced has not totally perished from the earth. If you open your eyes and your ears, you will still see and hear delightful experiences and accounts of that healthy child still alive in our midst.

To share a few examples: recently, my cousin told me about a family who went on vacation to Alaska. A young boy in the family, mesmerized by the night sky, asked, "Daddy, why don't we have stars like this at home?" His father explained that the brightness of the stars is hidden because of all the electric lights. The child became silent, deep in thought and then suddenly broke out of his pensive mood with this exclamation: *"I wonder what else we're missing!"* Indeed! What a wonderful insight for grown-ups to ponder. What are we missing?

Another story worth sharing concerns a child's wonderings about relationships. One of my friends shared an incident about her three-and-a-half-year-old niece. The little girl asked her aunt, "Do you have children?" "No," my friend replied. "Do you have a husband?" Again the answer was, "No." Once again the little girl persisted, "Do you have a pet?" Upon receiving another "No," the tone of her voice became quite concerned as she asked in a slightly anguished tone, *"Well, what do you have?"* Take note that the child's questions are all about being in relationship with someone. My friend, of course, has many friends and extended family members and is involved in purposeful organizations and meaningful projects. The small child cannot readily see or comprehend those connections. Thus she is perhaps worried about her aunt's happiness and is doing a little interrogation. This story does say something very precious about a child's concerns and observations as to what is important in life. Those few questions tell us much about the workings of that little mind.

In the Gospel of Luke, Jesus gives praise to God because what has been hidden from those with great learning has been revealed to mere children. Perhaps these bits of wisdom manifested in children are a result of that age-old blessing of Jesus still hovering over them, clothing them with the simple truth of who they are.

A rather humorous memory that depicts the innocence of children happened a long time ago. In a neighborhood clinic I watched a small child blessing people with the ointment of attentiveness and presence. While awaiting my turn to see the doctor, this child unknowingly blessed all of us as we waited. There was a kind of magical spontaneity as without pretension she went from person to person in the waiting room asking about their health and why they were there to see the doctor. The embarrassed mother tried to rescue us but it was too late. The little girl had stolen everyone's heart and no one seemed to mind the rather personal questions like, "Are you very sick?" or "Who is your doctor?" The crowning moment, however, came when she reached an elderly woman who had very gnarled and crippled hands. The child gathered up those hands, held them in her own small hands, looked the woman straight in the eye and said, *"My granny has hands like this and she says that when she dies, God will fix them."*

That which may seem inappropriate to adults is often second nature to a child. It may be, precisely, this innocence and naturalness that Jesus wants restored in us, so that when we come into the kingdom of God, no remnants of the false or artificial will remain in our lives.

I give you praise, Father, Lord of heaven and earth,
for although you have hidden these things from the wise and the
learned you have revealed them to the childlike. (Luke 10:21)

In this prayer of praise Jesus is rejoicing in the truth that it is the childlike ones who are able to grasp wisdom that is hidden in little things. It is not too late for us to touch the child within. We still have access to our childlike spirit. We can return to our original delight in life. We can still appreciate the little things that our adult ways sometimes smother. We can resurrect the child. This is what I am trying to say in my poem "Is there a lost child in you?"[3]

What pains me most
these days
is my inability
to reach back into my years
and touch the child I was.

And yet,
loving
living
stirring
deep within my soul
that child
lives on.

There are days
when
my adult ways
turn tasteless in my mouth
and the child of long ago
starts
pressing on my soul.

On days like that
I long to touch the child again
and let her take me by the hand
and lead me down
a path that has a heart
and show me all the things
that
I've stopped seeing
because I've grown
too tall.

Reflection and Prayer

- Can you remember something you learned from a child in the past month?

- Are you among those who have tried to change your children into little adults?

- As you keep alive the memory of Jesus blessing the children think of ways you can continue that practice today. For parents of small children, a bedtime blessing is recommended. For those of you without small children, pray for children across the world at the end of each day. Extend your hand to the four directions. Pray your own prayer of blessing or the one given below.

Jesus,

Look kindly on these children (name specific children) and upon all the children of the world. Let your blessing of love and protection fall on them like dew from the heavens. Make your home in the heart of every child. Bless also the lost child in the lives of those who have grown up too fast. Reveal to us the hidden wisdom that lives in every experience. Unveil our grown-up eyes and give us joy in the little things. Return us to our original love. **Amen.**

8. Little Lights along the Way

Prayerfully read Deuteronomy 8:1-20.

> *Remember how for forty years now the* LORD, *your God,*
> *has directed all your journeying in the desert. (v. 2)*

We begin our reflection by focusing on the word *remember*. *Remember* is a beautiful word. To remember can be the source of much healing. The Hebrew people are asked to remember Yahweh, their faithful companion on that long, arduous passage through the desert. They are to be mindful of the unfailing guidance they experienced in the wilderness. They are to keep and cherish the commandments. When they finally enjoy the treasures of the promised land, they are to remember that these gifts came from the hands of the One who guided them on that great and terrible journey. These bountiful blessings were not acquired through their own power. Thus, they are encouraged to remember; they are cautioned never to forget.

Remembering is a spiritual practice. We who have experienced our own wilderness journey can probably relate to the desert sojourn of our biblical ancestors. When things start looking brighter in our lives, it is easy to forget who companioned us through the hard times. We may even forget why we need the commandments when our own will wants to rule our lives. Remembering the source of our blessings is an important piece of our life's work.

There are times when we find ourselves looking at the commandments as a bother and a burden. At times such as these it could serve us well to notice how the Hebrew people deeply treasured the commandments. Keeping the commandments is not one-sided. The covenant works both ways and God's promise of faithfulness includes us also (Deut 7:9; 11:13-14). The Hebrew understanding and reverence for the law is considerably more potent than our feeble efforts in keeping the commandments. If the word *commandment* seems harsh and foreboding to us, perhaps we need to rethink the meaning of God's law. We don't just *keep the commandments*; the *commandments keep us*. They safeguard us. They are like little lights that help us stay on the right path. They are dependable guides for us on our spiritual journey. The intention of the law was to assist us in living lives of concern for one another. If we look at the commandments in this way, we will see that they are blessings. That is why I like to call them "little lights along the way." Like a torch, they light up our path. If we want to put ourselves on the path of life, then, we might make a practice of careful examination of the ways God wants to bless us.

In biblical tradition the law was so revered that the stone tablets Moses received on Mt. Sinai were carried in the ark of the covenant much like the way we entrust the Blessed Sacrament to our tabernacles. The great commandment (the Shema) was honored so deeply that the people were asked to bind these sacred words like an emblem or a bracelet, on their wrists, their foreheads, their doorposts (Deut 6:4). This may have been a metaphoric command but God's people took this quite literally and wore on their wrists and foreheads "phylacteries," boxes containing the sacred words of the law. Although this was a beautiful practice, the real challenge is getting the words into our hearts and making them a part of our lives.

Keeping all this in mind, then, we can understand more fully the lovely words of encouragement and admonition at the beginning of chapter 8 of Deuteronomy. The people are reminded of God's companionship with them on their journey through the wilderness. This is something they are to remember and never forget. Yahweh was with them on that long journey, directing and guiding, humbling them and checking out their heart's faithfulness. The manna they were fed was more than bread. It was the manna of the law.

They learned how to listen to their own ingenuity and creativity. Artists and craftspersons emerged from their ranks in order to help one another survive in the harsh desert. Surely this is the reason their clothes did not wear out and their feet were always shod (Deut 8:4). They learned how to serve one another. God took the *sometimes questionable* raw material of this incongruent group and formed them into a community. Perhaps that was the greatest of miracles.

For the LORD, *your God, is bringing you into a good country.*
(v. 7)

This good country with its streams of flowing water, its fruits and riches of many kinds, has been given to each of us. Spend some moments with verses 7 through 16 and ask yourself what these gifts are symbolic of in your life. Name the good country of your life: the riches that have come to you from the hand of God, and like the Hebrew people, bless the One who has been so gracious to you. There is grace in knowing from whom the grace has come.

A loving guardian, who is the source of our life, supports and guides us on our journey. Thus it may be helpful to remember that we are not guided by the starlight of our eyes alone. Neither are we supported by the staff of our ingenuity. Other eyes are keeping vigil with us on our pilgrimage. A source of strength greater than our own becomes our staff of support. This is what our biblical ancestors had to learn on their desert journey. This is what each of us must learn in the midst of daily life. God is our star and our staff. We work together.

Like the Hebrew people, we too enjoy a covenant relationship with God. This relationship was sealed with our baptism and validated in the sacrament of confirmation. There is nothing more precious that we can bring to this relationship than our faithfulness to the commandments, especially the Great Commandment of love. As our attitude toward the commandments is transformed into a deeper understanding of their value, we will more easily be able to recognize them as *little lights along the way.*

Reflection and Prayer

- Name some of your own wilderness journeys. How have you been led from slavery to freedom? Who have been your guides?

- Pray with the commandments in Exodus 20. Take each commandment and reflect on how it can be a light for your path.

- Reflect on God as your star and your staff.

O Star and Staff of My Life,

On my journey into the good country of my life you have lavished me with gifts and surrounded me with miracles. Such treasures have come from your hand, O my God. Thank you for your abiding presence on my wilderness journeys. You are my light! You are my support! Guide me with your law and teach me. Shine on the paths I must walk. Uphold me when I falter. Feed me with the Bread of your Word. Receive my love! Increase my love! **O Star and Staff of my Life—on you I have leaned since birth.**

Poetic Summary of Chapter Five

God Speaks

O Heart of My Heart: I sent you to this earth to be a blessing. Before mountains were born, I was aware of your goodness. Before rivers began flowing, I knew the yearning in your hearts. I embedded "eternity" in your souls so that you might lean toward me. I implanted my own life within you so that you might be drawn back to the source. I have observed your "comings and goings" on this earth and I love you. I have watched you love one another and I have covered you with blessings. I cherish your original love.

Original Love of My Life: You have lost some of your early love. Return to the source of that love; your ancestors are waiting. Return to your original love. Borrow my eyes and return! Borrow my heart and return! Borrow my feet and dance your way back into your early love. Your "inner child" will be your guide. She will lead you in the dance; he will dance with you. Grace will be your companion. Joy will be your bread for this homeward journey. Hope will be your nourishment.

We Speak

Original Love of Our Lives: We carry the mountains and rivers in our beings. We have belonged to you before we were born. You are the Star from which we gather our light. You are the Staff upon which we lean when we are weary. You are our star and our staff! Our dancing feet are ready; we are returning to our early love.

O Sunrise of Our Lives: In this new season of returning to our original love, light a lamp in our hearts. Let the tiny flame of our love take charge of our attitudes, revealing to us who we are and who we are becoming. May you be praised in the words, actions, and silences of our days. Teach us to praise and affirm one another. Affirmation is like the light that brightens our path; it cheers us into the dance. So give us the insight to encourage one another each day, saying, *"The sun is shining in the sky. Wake up! It is time to do good! It is time to return to our original love!"*

Notes

Introduction

[1] Pete Hamill, *Snow in August* (New York: Warner Books, 1997), 86.

Chapter One

[1] Rainer Maria Rilke, *Rilke's Book of Hours: Love Poems to God*, trans. Anita Barrows and Joanna Macy (New York: Penguin Group, 1996), 70.

[2] Dom Helder Camara, *The Desert is Fertile* (Maryknoll, NY: Orbis Books, 1974), 14.

[3] *The Cloud of Unknowing*, ed. William Johnston (Garden City, NY: Doubleday Image Books, 1973), 146.

[4] Paschal Botz, *Runways to God* (Collegeville, MN: Liturgical Press, 1980), ix.

[5] Christine Valters Paintner, *Water, Wind, Earth & Fire: The Christian Practice of Praying the Elements* (Notre Dame, IN: Sorin Books, 2010), 2.

[6] Sue Woodruff, *Meditations with Mechtild of Magdeburg* (Santa Fe, NM: Bear & Company, 1982), 10.

Chapter Two

[1] Roy Scheele, "A Gap in the Cedar," *Accompanied* (Crete, NE: Best Cellar Press, 1974). Used with permission.

[2] Laurens van der Post, *The Heart of the Hunter* (New York: William Morrow and Company, 1961), 235–37.

[3] Philip Zaleski and Paul Kaufman, *Gifts of the Spirit: Living the Wisdom of the Great Religious Traditions* (San Francisco: HarperSanFrancisco, 1997), 94.

[4] Quotations from Benedict's Rule are taken from *Rule of Saint Benedict 1980*, ed. Timothy Fry (Collegeville, MN: Liturgical Press, 1981).

Chapter Three

[1] Madeleine L'Engle, *Penguins & Golden Calves* (Wheaton, IL: Harold Shaw Publishers, 1996).

Chapter Four

[1] Mark Nepo, *The Exquisite Risk: Daring To Live An Authentic Life* (New York: Three Rivers Press, 2005).

[2] Demetrius Dumm, *Cherish Christ Above All: The Bible in the Rule of St. Benedict* (Mahwah, NJ: Paulist Press, 1996), 60–63.

[3] Johannes Baptist Metz, *Poverty of Spirit* (Mahwah, NJ: Paulist Press, 1968), 25.

[4] Rory Cooney, "Do Not Fear to Hope," *Change Our Hearts*, with Gary Daigle and Theresa Donohoo, Oregon Catholic Press, used with permission.

Chapter Five

[1] Ella Cara Deloria, *Waterlily* (Lincoln: University of Nebraska Press, 1988).

[2] Nikos Kazantzakis, *Report to Greco* (New York: Simon & Schuster, 1965), 44.

[3] Macrina Wiederkehr, *A Tree Full of Angels: Seeing the Holy in the Ordinary* (San Francisco: HarperCollins, 1988), 63, used with permission.

Bibliography

Binz, Stephen J. *Lectio Divina* Bible Study Series: *The Mass in Scripture, The Sacraments in Scripture,* and *Prayer in Scripture.* Huntington, IN: Our Sunday Visitor, 2011.

———. *Conversing with God in Scripture: A Contemporary Approach to Lectio Divina.* Ijamsville, MD: The Word Among Us Press, 2008.

Casey, Michael. *Sacred Reading: The Ancient Art of Lectio Divina.* Liguori, MO: Triumph Books, 1996.

Dumm, Demetrius. *Cherish Christ Above All: The Bible in the Rule of St. Benedict.* Mahwah, NJ: Paulist Press, 1996.

———. *Praying the Scriptures.* Collegeville, MN: Liturgical Press, 2003.

Funk, Meg. *Lectio Matters: Before the Burning Bush.* New York: Continuum, 2011.

Haase, Albert, OFM. *Living the Lord's Prayer: The Way of the Disciple.* Downers Grove, IL: InterVarsity Press, 2009.

Little Rock Catholic Study Bible. Edited by Catherine Upchurch; Irene Nowell, OSB; and Ronald D. Witherup, SS. Collegeville, MN: Liturgical Press, 2011.

Mulholland, M. Robert, Jr. *Shaped by the Word: The Power of Scripture in Spiritual Formation.* Nashville, TN: The Upper Room, 1983.

Painter, Christine Valters. *The Artist's Rule: Nurturing Your Creative Soul with Monastic Wisdom.* Notre Dame, IN: Ave Maria Press, 2011.

———, and Lucy Wynkoop, OSB. *Lectio Divina: Contemplative Awakening and Awareness.* Mahwah, NJ: Paulist Press, 2008.

Rule of Saint Benedict 1980. Edited by Timothy Fry. Collegeville, MN: Liturgical Press, 1981.

Rupp, Joyce. *The Cup of Our Life: A Guide for Spiritual Growth.* Notre Dame, IN: Ave Maria Press, 1997.

Svoboda, Melannie, SND. *Just Because: Prayer-Poems to Delight the Heart.* New London, CT: Twenty-Third Publications, 2010.

Wiederkehr, Macrina. *The Song of the Seed: A Monastic Way of Tending the Soul.* San Francisco: HarperSanFrancisco, 1995.

A Year of Sundays Series. Collegeville, MN: Liturgical Press.

Yeary, Clifford M. *Pilgrim People: A Scriptural Commentary.* Collegeville, MN: Liturgical Press, 2010.